Between Heaven and Charing Cross

Between Heaven and Charing Cross

Martin Warner

mowbray

Published by Mowbray, a Continuum imprint
The Tower Building, 11 York Road, London SE1 7NX
80 Maiden Lane, Suite 704, New York, NY 10038

www.continuumbooks.com

First published 2009

British Library Cataloguing-in-Publication Data
A catalogue record for this book is available from the British Library.

ISBN: 184706-538-4
ISBN: 978-184706-538-4

Typeset by BookEns Ltd, Royston, Herts.
Printed and bound by the MPG Books Group, Bodmin, Cornwall

Contents

	Acknowledgements	vii
	Introduction	1
1	Handling Reality	7
2	Knowledge and Nostalgia	33
3	Power Dressing	57
4	Binding Time	81
5	The Art of Celebration	107
	Conclusion	127

For my mother

Acknowledgements

This book began as a series of retreat addresses, first to students from The College of the Resurrection, Mirfield, and then to clergy from the Edmonton Episcopal Area in the Diocese of London. I am grateful to the retreatants for their companionship and good humour, and to the then Principal of Mirfield, Chris Irvine, and the Bishop of Edmonton, Peter Wheatley, for their invitations.

Subsequently, a number of preaching engagements have prompted me to flesh out those addresses; for that I am indebted to Carl Turner, Reg Bushau, Vick House, Norman Banks, Jeremy Dussek and Philip Mowbray.

Friends and colleagues have patiently read and re-read the script, or commented in other helpful ways. I, and you, have good reason to be grateful to them, especially to Robin Ward, Vanessa Baron, Jim Walters, Susan Knowles, Rachel Boulding and Ann Loades. Likewise, the genial encouragement and patience of Robin Baird-Smith, and the support of his colleagues at Continuum, should not go without recognition. I am also grateful to Antony Gormley for permission to use an image from his exhibition Blind Light on the cover.

Anthony Prescott preached at my first Mass in St Peter's, Plymouth about the hands of a priest. A former colleague of his, Sam Philpott, was my first vicar. He and his parish taught me the priesthood. In large measure this book is also the fruit of their wisdom and I am glad to have this opportunity to acknowledge that with gratitude.

Martin Warner
St Matthew, Apostle and Evangelist
2008

Introduction

Charing Cross features prominently in one of my earliest memories of London. My mother and I had been to see a film and were waiting at that station for the train home. On a bench opposite us was a large, recumbent figure, a woman, wrapped in all manner of newspapers, coats and clothing, snoring soundly. Suddenly she sprang a leak and a pool formed beneath her. My surprise was so great I was unable to speak, but remember looking anxiously at my mother, who remained quite calm, as though this sort of thing was typical of London life. Sadly, it was.

This experience has, ever since, posed in my mind the question of what it means to be human. Buried deep down within that bundle of cast-off wrappings, and even deeper, in the mind, heart, soul, self-knowledge, fear, hurt and hope of that human being, there lay an answer to the mystery of this question. Or, if not an answer, at least the story that would account for what she might say of herself and who she would hope to be.

In the later stages of growing up, I glimpsed something of a social gospel that sought to identify with those who were lost to the inclusive processes of society. This was not only an awareness of people with no homes; it also began to address the process by which they got to that state. My mother was among the first to join the Samaritans in the Medway towns, and the recognition of her sympathy for the human condition and her practical patience in responding to it quickly made her a leader in that fledgling organization. Issues of drug abuse, marital breakdown, and the fallout from being part of a society that in the 1970s was still seeking its identity in sexual freedom, and liberation from old patterns of class and education, combined to form an atmosphere of heady optimism tempered by profound disorientation and loss.

A formative experience for me was being a cathedral chorister. To it I owe, among other things, a respect for words and language, some sense of history (Rochester Cathedral was founded in 604 and the school attached to it not long after), an appreciation of the amazing skills of architects and artists, and what I hope is a healthy scepticism about the self-importance of cathedrals.

This was also where I was taught the Christian faith, and in that learning were sown the seeds of a vocation to the priesthood. Among my discoveries in the formation of that vocation was the enigmatic Roman Catholic poet Francis Thompson, through whom another aspect of the social gospel, one that was incarnational and sacramental, was articulated. Thompson was born in 1859 into a Roman Catholic convert family in Preston, Lancashire. After an education at Ushaw, Durham that gave him a love of Greek and Latin literature, Thompson was sent to Owens College in Manchester to learn medicine. In 1879 he gave up his studies there, moved to London, fell ill, and began a life cycle of illness, recovery, drug addiction, rescue by loving, Catholic friends, and the composition of visionary and sometimes sentimental poetry, and living rough on the streets. But Thompson's love of the ancient world informed his Christian faith and supplied the form and language of his writing.

It was Thompson's vagabond status in London that I first found most intriguing. The benches around Charing Cross are still inhabited by many who are homeless and destitute, lost for many different reasons in the complexity of life as they have been given it. These days, we might chat with some of them when buying the *Big Issue*. Scottish Andy and Terry are the two from whom I regularly get my copy, and in both cases there is a story to tell that reminds me of aspects of Francis Thompson's life.

'Foxes have holes, and birds of the air have nests: but the Son of Man has nowhere to lay his head.' (Matthew 8.20) It is this aspect of closeness to the experience of Jesus that I find most powerfully expressed in Thompson's poetry, particularly his poem 'The Kingdom of God', subtitled 'In No Strange Land'. The title of this book,

Between Heaven and Charing Cross, comes from that poem, and I shall quote it in full at the end of this introduction.

But first I want to connect Thompson's poetry with liturgy and the theological vision of the Roman Catholic Church as it was expanding in England during Thompson's life. It was the ordering of godly worship in Rochester Cathedral that fostered my fascination with this aspect of Christian history in England. The second half of the nineteenth century was a time of growing confidence for Roman Catholicism. Alongside the Tractarians in the Church of England it combined ministry to the poor with beauty in worship and serious engagement with the artistic life of the nation, in the work of Augustus Welby Pugin, for example.

The Roman Catholic Hierarchy had been re-established in England and Wales in 1850, and cathedrals were being built for its new dioceses. The star of the Tractarian movement in the Church of England, John Henry Newman, had made his submission to Rome and brought an intellectual edge to Catholicism that drew many followers. The London Oratory gave London Society an *entré* into Roman Catholicism, while the hymns of Father Faber began to filter popular Catholic devotion into the Anglican bloodstream.

Against the confidence of this revival of Catholicism in England, Thompson's poetry draws its strength from an implicit sacramentalism, energized by the celebration of the Eucharist. There is materiality in this vision. God and matter are not like oil and water. In the species of bread and wine, categories of temporal and eternal, physical and spiritual, coalesce in such a way as to enable people to see the sacramental presence of the body of Jesus Christ in the white disc of bread that is the host of the Eucharist. To the drug-dependent vagrant that Francis Thompson was, the celebration of the Mass was effortlessly understood as heaven come to earth.

This is where I come back to the woman on the bench at Charing Cross. If Thompson knew the reality of Jesus Christ who walked the streets with him, why should she not also have known it? If Thompson's experience of loss drew him closer to Jesus, who freely experienced the loss of all things for our enrichment, why should that bundled woman not be closer to the Lord of life than I could ever guess or imagine? If, against all the odds, Thompson clung to the hem of heaven, believing it to be his future, could not that woman also share a similar future – one that would also claim a dignity for her life here and now?

This hunch that street life and the sanctuary of God are intimates is what lies behind the structure of this book. When a priest goes to the altar to celebrate the Eucharist, prayers are provided for preparation and the putting on of each of the items of priestly vesture. The form of prayers I shall quote was codified in the late sixteenth century. Though they are now, sadly, no longer an obligatory requirement in the Roman Catholic Church, I suspect their use is spreading again in that communion, just as many in the Anglican Communion never abandoned the practice of using them.

The first prayer is for the washing of hands. Then comes a prayer for the amice, a square of cloth that originally covered the head while vesting, but now acts as a collar. Over this is placed the basic liturgical garment, a white tunic, called an alb, for which the third prayer is said. The fourth accompanies tying a rope girdle round the waist: this holds in place a broad piece of cloth that goes round the neck, the stole, over which sits the large chasuble, the top coat of a priest's or bishop's vesture; we shall put the prayers for these two items together, and allocate them a chapter, as we shall for each of the other four.

In each case the prayer, action or vestment addresses a part of our lives. Hands relate to dealing with the material world and our own material nature. The head is where we locate the mind and our thought processes. The basic garment, the alb, is a statement about dress code. The girdle signifies commitment. The stole and chasuble are indicative of celebration. These are the themes to which each of the prayers will turn our attention.

The focus of the book is not on priest-craft or, indeed, on liturgy as such. It is on how the fundamental aspects of being human that are associated with the vesting prayers connect life with Christian discipleship. So, for example, what might they say about the woman on the bench in Charing Cross? What about her hands, mind, dress, and the string that holds her clothing together? What do we say about her place in the celebration of the Eucharist, between Heaven and Charing Cross, at which Jesus, the homeless preacher from Nazareth, is her host?

Whether you know little about Christianity or are seeking renewed understanding of familiar ground, the chapters that follow are offered to encourage your further exploration of Christian faith, hope and love. Whatever their shortfalls, I hope they will contribute to a conviction that you, like every human being, have the capacity to apprehend heaven, even now on earth. I hope you will find renewal in joyful, Eucharistic celebration which reveals immortal life by means of mortal frailty.

I hope that, like Francis Thompson, you will see Jesus.

The Kingdom of God

In No Strange Land
O world invisible, we view thee,
O world intangible, we touch thee,
O world unknowable, we know thee,
Inapprehensible, we clutch thee!

Does the fish soar to find the ocean,
The eagle plunge to find the air –
That we ask of the stars in motion
If they have rumour of thee there?

Now where the wheeling systems darken,
And our benumbed conceiving soars! –
The drift of pinions, would we harken,
Beats at our own clay-shuttered doors.

The angels keep their ancient places; –
Turn but a stone, and start a wing!
'Tis ye, 'tis your estrangèd faces,
That miss the many-splendoured thing.

But (when so sad thou canst not sadder)
Cry; – and upon thy so sore loss
Shall shine the traffic of Jacob's ladder
Pitched betwixt Heaven and Charing Cross.

Yea, in the night, my Soul, my daughter,
Cry, – clinging heaven by the hems;
And lo, Christ walking on the water
Not of Gennesareth, but Thames!

Chapter 1

Handling Reality

Give strength to my hands, O Lord, and wash away every blemish
. . . that I might be ready to do your service.

'Let me see if your hands are clean; fingernails, too.' This was my
optician speaking, quite recently, when I'd asked about the possibility of having contact lenses as a way of avoiding varifocals. His words
brought back long forgotten echoes of childhood. Hand inspection
before meals was part of school life, implemented with slightly less
formality at home. But here was I, several decades later, being told, 'If
you want to see, you'll have to wash your hands – thoroughly!'

Part of me responded warmly to the idea of a connection between
the orderliness of clean hands and new vision. I liked the thought of
preparing for a kind of minor operation that was defined by the simple rules for putting in first one, then the second contact lens: always
starting with the right eye, always washing and rinsing the lenses as I
take them out, always washing my hands first.

Learning how to live and flourish within rules and order is part of
childhood. It introduces us to a process of socialization in which we
learn the patterns of life in an adult world, but also become capable
of seeing through the accumulated distortions of that world. This is
something that the film and recent musical in London's West End,
Mary Poppins, explores with beguiling naïvety.

As a governess Mary Poppins brings order to the lives of two
children, Michael and Jane, who have dysfunctional but impecca-
bly respectable parents. They have a father, George Banks, who is
consumed with subservient ambition for his career in a bank, and a
mother, Winifred Banks, frivolously besotted with the serious cause

of women's emancipation. Neither is doing very well at being a parent, or being themselves.

'A place for everything and everything in its place' is Mary Poppins' recipe for beginning to clean things up. But it isn't a bitter recipe: 'A spoonful of sugar makes the medicine go down,' she trills, as the children are swept up into a new routine of cleanliness and order. How does this connect with vision?

One of the children's outings with Mary Poppins involves an encounter with Bert, who is, among other things, a pavement artist drawing pictures in chalk. All four characters are told to join hands and jump into Bert's handiwork, a picture in chalk on the pavement that becomes a reality in their imagination and experience. Clean hands; ordered lives; structured drawing; inspirational instruction; the leap of faith; new vision: this is one way of reading the sequence of events that begins to transform the lives of the children and their parents.

As the story unfolds, it reveals further details that resonate with recent economic events. There is a financial crisis: the credibility of the bank where Michael's father works is called into question because Michael wants his tuppence back, and the old men of the bank won't cooperate; they want his money for profit. Rather than invest his tuppence in a bank, Michael insisted he wished to give it to the old woman on the steps of St Paul's, so that she could feed the birds. This inadvertently causes a run on the bank and Michael's father loses his job. This in turn forces a moment of crisis in which George Banks is confronted by the disarray of his priorities as a husband and parent.

What Mary Poppins had started in the nursery with her insistence on cleanliness and order ends with a new vision of human life and its potential quality. Freed from the tyranny of work and respectability, the Banks family become capable of spending time together in enjoyment. 'Let's go fly a kite' is the song of their finale, with the overtone, intentional or otherwise, of a speculative attitude to life, open to all its possibilities.

This story comes to us from the world of Disney and family entertainment, and it does not linger on the tough details of global economy, redundancy and social structures. But it does invite us to see a little way beyond the sentimental 'feel-good factor' of the musical, and it introduces us to the notion that clean hands, or at least hands that we are attentive to, can be the means by which new vision is opened to us.

In this chapter we shall explore how the relationship between hands and vision might work in the normal experiences of life. We shall look at how this affects us in key areas of life such as childhood, marriage, and engagement in society. We shall also consider how hands can function in the Christian tradition to reveal the vision of God. Ultimately, we shall note that the experience of the vision of God mediated through our hands is profoundly personal, bent into our own reach, as the poet Alice Oswald puts it.

But first we begin by looking at how some of the issues raised in *Mary Poppins* are dealt with more seriously by other, more recent writers. Imagination and family life are the two issues we begin with and the first of them takes us back into the theatre, to a play by Lee Hall entitled *The Pitmen Painters*.

Art Reveals your Soul

Art, music, dance, theatre, and all the technological wizardry that enhances our hand-dependent accomplishments, form the core curriculum of learning how to embark upon the adventure of being human. All too often this enterprise can seem to be the preserve of those who have the privilege of an education that provides the leisure to explore this adventure.

By contrast, Lee Hall's play *The Pitmen Painters* tells the story of miners in Ashington, just north of Newcastle, who demonstrated that imagination and the skill of painting – and painting well – is something intrinsic to being human; it is not determined by social class or status.

The story is that in 1934, due to a mix-up, the Workers' Education Association sent an art historian instead of an economic historian to give a series of evening lectures to a group of miners. The lecturer, Robert Lyon, confronted by a group who knew nothing about his points of reference, bravely invited the miners to begin to make their own art. The quality of the paintings and the strength of the subject matter established the national reputation of the Ashington Group, who continued to work as miners.

The first medium in which the group worked was linocuts. The task of cutting into the material from which the image is made emphasized a connection between the hard manual labour of the miners and the manual dexterity of their imaginative ability. The handiwork that subsequently emerged in their paintings continued to express this connection with their identity as manual labourers and as people whose hands hold other skills.

Lee Hall demonstrates that the visionary aspect of this work is not located simply in the pictures that the artists paint; it is also in the way they begin to regard themselves. In the play the most articulate of the artists is Oliver Kilbourn. Oliver describes how he worked on his first painting right through the night: 'And I was shaking – literally shaking – 'cos for the first time in my life, I'd really achieved something – I had made something that was mine, not for someone else – not for money – not for anything, really.'

There is an important point here about turning art and ultimately people into a commodity. Later in the play a wealthy patron, Helen Sutherland, introduces the Ashington Group to the artist Ben Nicholson, whom she has been funding, but then announces that she is moving away from the area. She tells Oliver that the Nicholson paintings are beginning to fetch a good price, and one realizes with chilling clarity that something free and live (imagination and artistic skill, in this instance) can also be quantified by commercial transaction.

The pitmen painters are, of course, all too well aware of the necessity of earning a living, whether as artists or as miners. But the nature of their approach to art as the means by which their hands liberate their spirits gives them a simple and compelling eloquence. Oliver Kilbourn understands this perfectly: 'art is making things possible that weren't there before'. By this he means that art is not simply a record of what is actually seen, like in a photograph; it is a statement of what is seen and is not seen, the unseen being what is potential, or implied, or held invisibly in the memory of the artist, of the subjects painted, or of the viewer. He sums this up later on: 'It's like what Ben Nicholson says: spirituality and painting are the same thing.'

Lee Hall is well known for writing the story of Billy Elliot, the lad who danced his way to freedom out of the dark conflicts of the miners' strike in the 1980s. In *The Pitmen Painters* Hall has returned to this theme of transformation, this time through handiwork, not footwork. As the artists Jimmy, George and Oliver explain at the end of Act One, 'You take one thing – and you make one thing into another – and you transform – who you are.'[1]

As human beings we need to remain capable of constructing an imaginative world, forming relationships that guarantee dignity and hope, and protecting our collective and individual memory. Working as a priest in the inner-city areas of Plymouth and Leicester, I used to reflect on what the greatest challenge was in my life and ministry. The answer, I think, was the challenge to sustain the imagination, in myself and in those among whom I lived.

Sustaining the imagination was one of the reasons why work with young people in those parishes seemed to be so important and refreshing. It was an invaluable stimulus to the imagination, in finding ways to communicate, and in understanding the swiftly changing culture of language that young people use and reinvent with amazing facility. It taught me that if as adults we allowed the imagination to flag, not only would we be inhibited in our understanding of any social world different from our own; we would undoubtedly be poorer at the task of understanding heaven.

Imagination is crucial to the enterprise of faith. If we cannot imagine this life as different from the way it is, but just as real, we shall find it almost impossible to imagine ourselves and others as lightning-rods of the Holy Spirit, catalysts of conversion, or subversive agents of justice and peace. More pressingly, perhaps, without imagination we may simply find it difficult to understand why God loves us or, to put it another way, to understand that we are worth loving and so can learn to love ourselves.

Imagination is also one of the agents necessary for the recognition of our similarity to each other. Janet Martin Soskice explores this theme in a recent collection of essays entitled *The Kindness of God*.

The book's introduction explains the significance of the title, pointing out that in Middle English 'to say that Christ is "our kinde Lord" is not to say that Christ is tender and gentle, although that may be implied, but to say that he is kin – our kind'.[2]

Soskice makes a strong case for understanding the human and spiritual importance of the practical processes of parenting, and it is here that we come to the second theme raised by *Mary Poppins*, the nature of family life, but especially of parenting. This is often about literally hands-on tasks, such as cooking a meal, wiping a bottom, or giving a bath. Reflecting on this, Soskice observes:

> Most women in general, if not every woman in particular, have been concerned with the management of ordinary life and the realm of necessity. And most mothers – and indeed, attentive fathers – realize that there is something inchoately graced about these dealings.[3]

Perhaps children intuitively recognize the working of this grace in the symbol of the parental hand. Tackling the hand is one of the most obvious ways you attract attention, pulling and shaking and refusing to let go: 'Pleeeease can we have more ice cream, another ten minutes, a Wii', etc. But it is precisely in the extent to which the parental hands express a practical, unsentimental, but profoundly loving attentiveness that something about the nature of being kin, being kind, being like God, is communicated to our children.

The challenge of preparing children for adulthood is not simply about what they, the children, should do or be like, but about what we, the adults, should do and be like. The experience of childhood that should prepare them for adulthood is that of living with adults who attend to what is happening in every aspect of life around them.

In this regard attention is an extension of the world of play and imagination. It is a 'hands-on' activity because there can be no substitute for the person whose attention is sought. A message on your blog or a text on the mobile phone can suggest to your children your real interest in them, but only your hands, eyes, ears, mouth and arms, as the instruments of your attention, can convincingly articulate 'kindness'.

In this respect, the relationship between Jesus and God, described so often in parental terms, becomes a paradigm for us of what adulthood should be like. To grow up into Christ, to realize the dignity of our adoption as the most loved children of God, is to step into the relationship of utter attentiveness that exists between the persons of the Trinity.

One of the great revelations of this attentiveness was given to Abraham by the oaks of Mamre (Genesis 18.1–8). Abraham is himself attentive to the needs of the three strangers, in whom the Christian Church has seen the figures of God, Father, Son and Holy Spirit. Abraham prepares a calf, while Sarah makes cakes, indicating the sacred quality of a meal as something in which the produce of the earth is the gift of God and worthy of being offered to God as the sign of our thanks and praise. In the prayers that the Christian Church has taken from her Jewish origins, we give thanks for bread, 'which earth has given and human hands have made' and for wine, 'fruit of the vine and the work of human hands'. Here, again, our hands become the means by which, as the pitmen painters put it, one thing is made into another, from which comes transformation.

We have considered the symbolic power of hands as the means by which we learn to relate to ourselves and to each other in the context of family relationships. This arose from our reflections on two aspects of the film and musical *Mary Poppins*. But staying with the wider scope of the relationship between our hands and our apprehension of the world around us, we are going to pursue further the social dimension of the fruits of our handiwork. Taking a cue from the Abraham story above, we look at the significance of the production of food and a meal, the labour of our hands, as something that also has transforming capacity in a variety of contexts.

Holding your Life in your Hands

Questions about how we handle our environment can seem so monumentally large that they are beyond us. But we do also know that some aspects of the management of sustainability lie in quite simple and immediate ways within the grasp of our own hands. It is extraordinary, for example, that at the moment when we seem to eat an increasing amount of pre-prepared food, the cult of the celebrity chef has reached epic proportions. The message of Jamie Oliver, Hugh Fearnley-Whittingstall and Valentine Warner (no relation), for example, is that good food is prepared by hand – your own hands.

Some will push this further and suggest that our food should also be grown and produced that way. Increasing awareness of the importance of fairly traded, sustainably produced, locally sourced food, in contrast to the carbon cost of kiwi fruit from New Zealand, for example, leads us to an appreciation of the hands that are responsible for the products that feed us.

In a recent trawl for caterers who might tender for the catering franchise at St Paul's there was no difficulty in selecting candidates for whom the issue of connection with hands that produced the ingredients of the food on offer was paramount. Fish from sustainable sources, landed at St Ives; the fairly traded Union Hand Roast Coffee company; jams made in Deptford, South London, from fruit grown by farmers in Kent: these were all examples cited by competing caterers of their policy towards a reconnection with the produce of the earth that is identifiably the work of our hands.

Reconnection with the environment is expressed by an increasingly popular interest in the hands that grow and produce our food. But the debate about food does more than demand our attention to sustainability; it also focuses attention on ourselves. Lack of exercise and a poor diet are among the reasons for a dramatic increase in obesity and consequent disease. We have to face the fact that the factors in this mix are invariably linked to economic indexes, as I discovered when working in an inner-city housing estate in Leicester.

The estate was an area of wide-ranging need, of brittle pride and sharp divisions. Many of the residents were teenage, single mums, living on benefits. As a governor of the local primary school, I was privileged to witness the outstanding commitment of the teaching staff to their catchment area. They sought to foster in children and their parents a sense of self-worth, often in the face of the significant odds that were stacked against those families and their flourishing.

One of the most instructive lessons I learned came from the

description of her life by a young mother of two children. She told us about the flat in which she lived and the two flights of stairs to get to it. She described getting a pram and a toddler up the stairs – there was no lift. She itemized her timetable after dropping the older child off at school and she gave us a breakdown of how long it took to shop for the cheapest food at the discount supermarket, which was on the other side of town. The end product, and a triumph in the face of considerable obstacles, was the arrival home from school of her older child and the provision of tea – chips, and beans on toast.

Here was a mum who survived a routine that would have defeated me had it been all that I could foresee on my future horizon. The meal that she produced for her children held within it something of the quality of transformation, in straightforward social terms. It was the triumph of determination over circumstance, the expression of parental optimism for her children, an outworking of commitment on which our understanding of God's staying with us is built.

The hands of this Leicester mum told the story of her life in two distinct ways. The first was physical: her nails were bitten to the quick and her fingers stained by nicotine. This was a statement of fragility, life as a high-wire act, and the use of any reasonable means available (cigarettes) to sustain it. The second message came from her handwriting. This was strong and neat; it was an indication of something, somewhere in her history, education and character, that her present situation had thwarted in its development. Helping teenage mums to fulfil their potential through raising self-esteem and sustaining them in employment was often the greatest contribution the school could make towards helping their children to thrive.

In October 2006 a government report indicated that out of 535,000 five-year-olds, 91,000 could not write simple words or hold a pencil. The point of mentioning this is not to apportion blame or deplore educational standards. But it is a statistic that says something about what significance we can and should attach to the capacity to pick up a pencil and write. Does our handwriting say something about ourselves that communicates a sense of dignity and self-knowledge? Isn't handwriting a statement about something human and live, in contrast to the de-personalized communication of e-mail and mobile phone text?

I realize that this can be a subjective and misleading form of assessment. But I was also struck recently by the importance an interview panel in the City of London attached to a handwritten letter of application, as distinct from the computer generated CV and other documents. The selection of a person for a particular job requires an assessment of character and personality as much as it requires a guarantee of capacity and experience. In the midst of a world that is heavily dependent on IT and the harsh, competitive terms of trade, it seemed that alertness to the human dimension of a person, manifested in handwriting, was a strong bid for extricating the unique freedom of personality from technical function.

This view is, of course, very heavily conditioned by our own time and history in which reading and writing, regarded as norms of educational attainment, are also taken to be indicative of a person's ability. Looking back at the history of education, however, we discover that the registers in which people signed the record of their marriage provide important evidence of the trends in literacy among women and men. There is evidence to suggest that it was the Industrial Revolution that brought about a discernable improvement in literacy levels. Taking 1760 to 1840 as accepted dates for the great expansion of industry in Britain, Edwin West has shown that '1790 is the date when the long term stability in male literacy changed to one of definite improvement.'[4]

Prior to the availability of free education, literacy is not an entirely reliable indication of intelligence, dignity and self-worth. But we ought to note that higher levels of affluence in the nation as a whole did improve literacy levels for women and men, and so opened up an enhanced access to social and cultural life. Taking your pen in your hand to write your signature was an expression, albeit a very simple one, of that access.

Signing the register is not the only way in which the involvement of hands in the celebration of marriage is symbolic of our personal and social identity. The symbolism of joining hands is also an ancient expression of the rite of marriage, though not an exclusively Christian one.

In a survey of Roman funerary monuments, Melissa Barden Dowling identifies a group that she calls clemency-marriage sarcophagi. These were particularly popular in the second half of the second century and so are contemporary with the spread of Christianity while it was still a forbidden religion. The carvings on these sarcophagi illustrate marriage in the portrayal of the nobleman, whose burial place it is, joining hands with his wife and being blessed by Eros, the god of love, and Juno, *regina*, queen of the State and the goddess of marriage and childbearing.[5]

That is not the only influence on the Christian rite of marriage in the joining of hands. There is a suggestion of it in the book of Tobit (8.12–13), one of the deutero-canonical books of the Old Testament, and it is certain that Jewish rites of marriage influenced parts of the early Church. The custom of the joining of hands as characteristic of the Christian rite of marriage was certainly known by the third century in the Christian Church and it is part of Anglican and Roman Catholic marriage rites today.

This focus on the joining of hands is emphasized by the exchanging of rings. Here the ritual focus on hands that are joined together and marked by the giving of rings alludes to revealing a new dimension in the world. The words spoken in the rite of marriage are precise and profound: 'All that I am I give to you, and all that I have I share with you.'

No statement of participation could be more absolute; it is a description of entering a new territory in which what I am and have is yours, and yours is mine. The territory is about more than my body and yours, just as it is about more than either of us might own, earn, inherit or squander. With my hands I have given you my history and my future and I have received yours.

This territory is more than an economic contract; it is about the space within which a new relationship will grow. In the Orthodox tradition, in which there are no vows as such, the crowns held over the couple are an expression of the new domain of marriage in which they jointly rule and order their lives. Even more explicitly, the Jewish marriage, which does involve vows and the exchanging of rings, takes place underneath a canopy, a *hupa*, which represents the new enclosure of the couple's home and life together.

To a large extent this use of hands is a kind of role-play. But it is an effective one, bringing something new into existence. Hands are used to express the new union that the mind, the will, the whole person intends to bring into existence with his or her spouse.

The crowns and the canopy of Orthodox and Jewish marriage rites make a striking statement about the environment of marriage. They both define the space that is the human person, emotional space as well as physical, bodily space, and the space in which we live – our home, street, town and land. This union, brought about by the joining of hands, also indicates a similarity between ourselves as embodied persons, and the earth. Both are a form of territory.

We understand this when we use the term 'space' to refer to something that is essentially the me that is my body and the me that is my intellectual, emotional self. So the phrase 'invading my space' is often a reference to my body space, while the phrase 'give me a bit of space' generally refers to my emotional self.

These examples have shown us how our hands not only tell a story, in tell-tale signs of bitten nails and nicotine stains, but in the ritual of marriage they make a story into reality. We use our hands to produce the fruits of the earth and a meal, with all the social and symbolic implications that can have. In a similar way we use our hands to produce new and invisible characters in our lives. We speak of signing away our lives in a contract; we transform our lives in the bond of marriage.

If the potential for all this rests in our human hands, how might it also rest in the hands of Jesus, who is fully human and fully God? We ought not to be surprised to discover that the gospels, and artists who similarly narrate his life, turn their attention to the hands of Jesus. What follows is a brief exploration of their treatment of how the hand can be the means by which we see who Jesus really is.

The Handwriting of God

A connection between the truth about ourselves and the handwriting of God is made in the story that we find in John's gospel about Jesus and the woman accused of adultery. It is a curious passage that does not really fit anywhere in the four gospels but has been inserted into the beginning of the eighth chapter of John's gospel.

A group of hostile male witnesses bring a woman to Jesus and accuse her of adultery. Jesus says nothing. He 'bent down and wrote with his finger in the ground'. The Pharisees press him and he responds, 'Let anyone among you who is without sin be the first to throw a stone at her.' And they go away, one by one, until only Jesus and the woman are left.

A story in which Jesus' enemies try to catch him out and thereby reveal their duplicity resonates with other stories in the gospels and suggests that this belongs to an authentic tradition. But there is scant evidence until the twelfth century that it was ever known as part of John's writing. It is an anomaly, like finding a chapter that has been torn out of a book and has no reference to the book's title.

What is the significance of Jesus writing in the dust of the ground? As with literacy levels in pre- and post-industrial Britain, it represents more than simply an ability to write. It speaks about the scope of personal identity and the capacity to bring about something of significance that is beyond oneself. The finger is a potent expression of this capacity.

The regulations in the Old Testament book of Leviticus describe how the priest should offer the sacrifice that atones for sins and that consecrates. The instructions repeatedly direct that the priest uses his finger to manipulate the blood of the sacrifice: this is the means by which something transformative happens. In the story about Jesus and the accused woman, the finger of his hand will reveal the inauthentic claim of the woman's accusers to be standard-bearers of truth and justice. It will also reveal the transforming authority of Jesus as one in whom justice and mercy meet, and who brings freedom from shame and hurt for those who are powerless.

The divine handwriting is something that the Old Testament uses to indicate the power of truth and judgement. In the book of Daniel, the story of Belshazzar's feast centres upon the appearance of the fingers of a human hand that write graffiti on the palace wall and then disappear. Daniel interprets the sign. Belshazzar has been using the sacred vessels of the Temple for his banquet, oblivious to their significance. Daniel is concise in his verdict: 'the God in whose power is your very breath, and to whom belong all your ways, you have not honoured. So from his presence the hand was sent and this writing was inscribed.' This last sentence could almost be prophetic of the story inserted into John's gospel.

Earlier in the Old Testament, in the story of the Exodus, one of the foundational moments of God's revealing of the code of truth and justice is characterized by the divine handwriting. Exodus 34.1 (and Deuteronomy 4.13) states it was the hand of God that wrote the ten commandments on the two tablets of stone. It is not uncommon for the Old Testament to think of God as intervening decisively in human affairs by his own hand. When the book of Exodus describes how Moses and Aaron are imposing the plagues on Egypt, the magicians of Pharaoh declare, 'It is the finger of God.' And this sense of the power of the hand or the finger of God features in a similar situation of conflict in the New Testament.

This conflict is recorded in Luke's gospel. It is about whether the power of a miracle that Jesus had worked is divine or demonic. Some people were saying that Jesus cast out demons by Beelzebul, the ruler of demons. Jesus challenges them: 'Now if I cast out the demons by Beelzebul, by whom do your exorcists cast them out? Therefore they will be your judges. But if it is by the finger of God that I cast out the demons, then the kingdom of God has come to you.' (Luke 11.19–20)

The action of Jesus in writing on the ground with his finger is symbolic of his personal identity as someone of divine authority who unmasks and who liberates. Jesus is not simply another person. When he writes he reveals that he is also God.

The response of Jesus to the woman who had been hideously treated in order to catch him out is a revelatory moment, rather like that of his tears at the tomb of Lazarus. There Jesus reveals both human and divine natures: he weeps and he raises new life. Here Jesus expresses compassion and intense sensitivity towards a woman whose life has been torn in shreds. These are very human qualities. But Jesus also restores her dignity and sets her free from condemnation. His encounter with her is re-creative, a moment when the handiwork of God in creation is re-revealed because what was damaged is shown to have been given new beauty and life.

Although we do not know what Jesus wrote on the ground, the outcome of it was a gift of human flourishing in the present/future dimension that is called the Kingdom of God and that swirls around Jesus as the atmosphere of his presence. A further signpost to that dimension is located in the subtle wording of the body language of Jesus in the story.

The action of crouching down to write on the ground is an impressive one. It instantly undermines the construct of the moral indignation paraded by his enemies. Just as impressive is the strength of the word that is used for Jesus standing up. Again there is a connection with Luke's gospel as the only other place where this word is used. In Luke, Jesus is talking about the point at which all things come to their fulfilment, and time and mortality are no more. That moment is described as the coming of the Son of Man with power and great glory. When it happens, 'stand up and raise your heads, because your redemption is drawing near,' says Jesus (Luke 21.28).

In the imaginative world of the artist the dynamic finger of God that is revealed in the hand of Jesus is what raises people up, both in the ministry of his incarnate life on earth and in the life to come of which the incarnation is the prelude. This is graphically demonstrated in two paintings by Caravaggio, both of which deal with resurrection but in different ways.

The first, and more obvious, is a painting of the resurrection of Lazarus. It's a late work, painted in about 1608, two years or so before Caravaggio's own death. In it Jesus stands on the left of the canvas and simply lifts his right hand towards the dead and naked body of his friend. The hand of Jesus is entirely passive, his index finger raised slightly above the others because that's the way the muscles and ligaments of the hand work. From behind him light pours onto the dead Lazarus, whose body is held in cruciform pose. Only one part of Lazarus seems to respond to the light: his right hand, which is lifted as though to respond with appreciation to an intense warmth that unfreezes him from death.

There is something fantastically understated about this interaction. The dynamics of resurrection rest in identity and intention, not demonstrative activity. The divine hand of Jesus elicits response from the deathly hand of Lazarus because heart speaks to heart in love.

A similar dynamic exists in the second painting by Caravaggio that uses exactly the same pose of the hand of Jesus. This rather better-known painting is of the call of Matthew. It is in the church of St Luigi, on the tourist route of central Rome. Jesus stands on the right of the picture and again the light comes from behind him to fall on the main subject of the scene, Matthew the tax collector. He is depicted as a young man who is bored witless by his life. His head sinks in heavy depression over that table at which he sits, surrounded by friends and colleagues. The hand that Jesus extends towards Matthew is in exactly the same poise as that extended towards Lazarus.

Here the artist has caught exactly the mood of Luke's comment about raising your head, and applied it to a scene of vocation in which the hand of Jesus extends a re-creative power that is not physical, as in the resurrection of Lazarus, but psychological. It is not therapy that Matthew needs, but purpose and new vision.

In a story that deals more explicitly with sight, John records that Jesus uses his hands to anoint with mud the eyes of a blind man, instructing him then to wash in the pool of Siloam, and the man regains his sight. It is another moment of transformation that is more than physical. The blind man recovers sight, but also sees Jesus for who he really is: 'He said, "Lord, I believe." And he worshiped him.' (John 9.38) Faith and transformation of personhood come from the hand of the incarnate Son of God: in his hand immortal life is revealed through, and in, mortal frailty.

How do we handle all this? How daring might we be in allowing our fears to be taken by God and reshaped? Would we ever reveal to God or anyone else our mean and tawdry secrets without being forced to by the trauma of public exposure? The invasive eye of the media is something that is constantly under discussion in our society today. But perhaps more instructive for us is the honest integrity with which artists reveal themselves by their own hands. A revelation of themselves by their own hand is also characteristic of the way in which Christians approach Jesus. A description of how that might be so is to be found in what I think is one of Stanley Spencer's most thoughtful paintings in his series 'Christ in the Wilderness'.

A Nail in the Hand

A telling connection between hands and the enclosure of marriage might be evident in the work of the twentieth-century artist Stanley Spencer. Spencer married his first love, Hilda Carline, in 1925 and they had two daughters, Shirin and Unity. By the early years of the following decade the marriage had foundered and Spencer had begun an infatuation with another woman, Patricia Preece, whom he married in 1937. That second marriage was an emotional catastrophe, in part due to Patricia's attachment to another woman, Dorothy Hepworth, but also because Spencer was still in love with Hilda.

In 1938 Spencer's life seemed to crash. He left Cookham and threw himself upon the kindness of friends in London, who found a room for him near Primrose Hill. The year or so that Spencer spent there was like a retreat in which he sought to restore some spiritual and religious integrity to his life. 'I was, as it were, in a wilderness,' he recalled in his diary in 1946, seeking a recovery from the recent vortex of lust and emotional turmoil. It was here that he worked on 'Christ in the Wilderness', a series of nine paintings, intended for the ceiling of Cookham church.

One painting in this series is entitled *The Scorpion*. It shows the large figure of Christ, seated, with a venomous scorpion cupped in his two meaty hands. The scorpion's dance of fury seems to be a distillation of the storms that Spencer had passed through. Hands that had twice signed marriage registers, that had sought but lost the enclosure of hoped-for domestic union, now painted the hands of Christ himself in which something of the potential for pain in this world is held but is not destroyed. Within that scorpion there was also life, and Spencer had seen 'Christ giving the once-over' of love to all things living, even the creepy-crawly things, in his wilderness experience.

The symbolism of hands takes on a variety of applications in this painting. The reference to marriage and heartbreak may or may not be intentional. The strong, sustaining, creative gentleness of God is clearly evident in Spencer's work and imagination in this picture. This was his material meditation on the words of Jesus to his disciples in St Luke's gospel and the mysterious application of them to contemporary life: 'See I have given you authority to tread on snakes and scorpions, and over all the power of the enemy; and nothing will hurt you. Nevertheless, do not rejoice at this, that the spirits submit to you, but rejoice that your names are written in heaven.' (Luke 10.19–20)

Spencer's image is a redemptive one. Destructive power is to be trodden underfoot by the disciples, but Jesus, the lord of life, saves and cherishes in his hands the life of the scorpion whose nature is to sting. The scorpion is not intentionally malevolent; it is itself. Jesus teaches the disciples that joy lies in the attainment of heaven, not in the exercise of authority. Similarly, Spencer finds joy in his wilderness recovery of the balance of his mind and renewed openness to God, though he continued to struggle with the demons within him that threatened that renewed intuition of heaven.

Holding the sting of life within our hands is no easy matter, particularly when we think of the consequences that have followed from doing so. The signing of the Munich Treaty by Nazi Germany, France, Britain and Italy in the early hours of 30 September 1938 would be one catastrophic example that unfolded all too swiftly into world war in the hands of those who had held the pens that signed the Treaty. And so it has been throughout history.

At the end of *The Mission*, a film of the novel by Robert Bolt, the Pope's Visitor-General, Fr Altamirano, reads a report of the destruction of the Jesuit missions in eighteenth-century South America. The Portuguese Captain-General, Senhor Hontar, attempts to justify the carnage that resulted from Fr Altamirano's signature on the order to close the missions. '"You had no choice. You must work in the real world. And the real world is thus." "Oh no," said Altamirano. "Thus have we made it."'

'Thus have we made it' are words, heavily laden with the realization of bitter consequences, that offer a good description of how we might reflect on the environment we inherit, what we do with it, and how we live our lives within it. We turn now to look in more detail at what this means for the use of our hands in worship.

'Hands that Holy Things Have Taken'

We have considered the material impact of our hands upon the world in the management of its resources for our food; we have seen it also in our ability to sign our commitment to the covenant of marriage in which our lives are formed. And, in the fusion of the material and the emotional aspects of our lives, we see in Spencer's handiwork the material expression of his own emotional condition. But what about the handling of our own lives in ways that allow ourselves to be open to God and transformed by God?

One of the great privileges of being a priest or Eucharistic minister is the giving of communion to the people of God. Preparing people to receive communion for the first time is a wonderful reminder of just how much it means to get up from your seat and come forward to receive, under the forms of bread and wine, the body and blood of Jesus Christ in the Eucharist. Part of the privilege for those who administer communion is in 'reading' the lives of communicants in the hands that they present and hold before you as the throne in which Jesus Christ is to be placed.

My own sense of how profound this could be was awakened by seeing, at the time of communion, the hands of a woman who was probably in her late fifties. She was a person of slight build and few words but the vitality of her life danced in her eyes. Her life was tough: she was the sole carer for a son who suffered from acute depression, could not work, lived at home, and had several times attempted to take his own life. When she came to receive communion she presented hands that were as rough and calloused as those of any workman. What kind of heavy-duty work this woman was doing in order to maintain her life and that of her son, I did not know, but I suspected that it was some kind of unremitting cleaning or laundry work.

Placing into the hands of this woman the body of Jesus was an extraordinary experience. It was as though one were consciously giving her the body of another son whose life would be taken from him by cruel circumstance, but at the same time it was a son whose life would be restored in the glory of resurrection. This resurrection life would be the sign of a new creation into which baptism already admits us, even while we live out our time in this old and mortal life.

It is Stanley Spencer's image of Jesus and the scorpion that informs this communion image in my mind. In Spencer's painting it seems as though the hands of Jesus are in fact open to receive communion – communion with the experience of being human, complete and entire. And when Jesus holds the scorpion it prefigures the nails that are the expression of our mark upon the God-made-flesh.

We commented earlier on the damaging consequences of the exploitative invasion of children's lives by the adult world. In mid-nineteenth-century Britain this theme was related explicitly to the wounds of the passion on the childhood hands of Jesus. Charles Dickens was famously outraged by John Everett Millais' painting entitled *Christ in the House of his Parents*, declaring that 'it showed the lowest depths of what is mean, repulsive, and revolting'. In one respect Dickens was right. The picture shows Joseph looking tenderly at the hand of the boy Jesus, who has cut himself; it is an artistic conceit that refers forward to the cross.

We might find that a rather sentimental take on the Christian story. But the marking of our lives upon the hands of Jesus is precisely the point of communion between the human and the divine that happens in the incarnation. And since it is of the very nature of communion that exchange is what takes place, Jesus also marks upon us, even in our depression, lostness, and despair, the potential for glory.

The importance of this for people of all ages should not be underestimated. The sense of placing oneself in the hands of Jesus to be sufficiently strengthened simply to stay alive is a serious proposition, especially for some young people. The terrifying levels of suicide among the young is evidence of this and the reasons for it are varied and complex.

One possible cause was brought home to me when a young parishioner rocked himself with sobbing and relief on coming to terms with the discovery that he no longer wished to commit suicide because he was gay. After the tough struggle of school, college, and establishing himself in a professional career, he had begun slowly to believe that a future life was possible.

Many a spiritual director and parish priest will have had the experience of conversation with a person who, like Spencer's Christ, is holding in his or her hands the turmoil of sexual confusion, betrayal and despair. In this situation I think that the image of childhood hands is helpful, because it reminds us that adults are also tender, child-like, manipulative, vulnerable and lovable. Imprisonment of our freedom comes in various forms, each of which demands its own means of liberation.

Although our attention to the deceptive infection of self-interest and greed demands that we always name those evils, we ought never to do so when the sentient hand of the child-within-the-adult still has the chance of calling the adult back to a recovery of trust and vulnerability. Here was a young man recovering courage, taking back his life into his own hands.

An important stage of that childhood recovery is liberation from guilt. It is here that the Church's ministry of the laying-on of hands can have a significant affect. This action expresses liberation from sins and wounds inflicted on us. The sealing of this action with the anointing of oil is a sign of strengthening and protection. After abuse, of whatever kind, the touch of this sacramental sign is the invitation to trust again, and to believe that human contact, with all its physical potential, can and should be beautiful, sacred and life-enhancing.

The role of our hands has been seen, once again, in what we build and shape, and in who we become. In the case of Stanley Spencer, painting was how he articulated his quest for calm, for escape from the world of emotional toil that he had made. But painting is not the only work of art through which the hands can liberate.

Time and Eternity in your Hands

The outer and the inner parts of who we are emerge through the hands in particularly distinctive ways for those who are deaf and communicate through signing. Perhaps even more distinctive is signing for people who are both deaf and blind. Each year when I worked at the Shrine of Our Lady of Walsingham the St John's Guild brought people who communicated through sign language. It was one of the specialist pilgrimages I looked forward to most, because these pilgrims had a grace about their communication that it was beyond my ability to emulate.

In large measure that grace was an expression of the patience and generosity of carers and signers who came on the pilgrimage. Their ministry as bridge-builders between different worlds of social interaction was itself an amazing form of communication. In particular, I was entranced by the unselfconscious ministry of the woman who signed in the hand of a person who was blind and deaf. The tactile nature of this communication made spoken words seem angular and lumpish in comparison. Their signed language, however, took on an almost sculptured quality as words were shaped and pressed into the flesh.

There are various ways in which the use of sign language has a liberating quality to it. The most obvious is that it tells people what everyone else is hearing. But it also permits response. It was some time before I noticed a group of people participating in perfect pitch and time when singing a hymn in the silent key of sign language. The statement it made was profound: sign language is social, it is praise, it is witness.

People who are deaf still live in society; that's the sign of being human. And those who do have hearing ought to be aware of the grace and beauty of the social world beyond that of our sound-dependent world. But hands that liberate from isolation into society have a particular significance when used for communication in prison.

In 2007 the General Synod of the Church of England debated a report entitled 'Taking Responsibility for Crime'. The debate was impressive for a number of reasons, but among the most memorable was the story a member of Synod told about visits to a Young Offender Centre. This visitor was going to sign for a young man in the Centre who was deaf. Eventually she was approached by some of the other inmates, who asked whether they could learn sign language so that they also could communicate with him. The result was a period of training for them that resulted ostensibly in the liberation of one deaf man from an additional social exclusion that was beyond the intention of his sentence. But there was more to the achievement than that.

An important aspect of this liberation was the whole process of responding to the special needs of another person. We can, too glibly, describe as 'disabled' those people who offer us in a unique way the opportunities for escape from our own destructive selfishness. The inmates who learned signing developed a skill and confidence that provided them with something positive and beneficial to take out of prison. Perhaps it was something that might lead eventually to employment and a whole new life.

Conclusion

In this survey of hands it has begun to emerge that what we might regard as simply and obviously symbolic often contains within it the indication of something more complex and mysterious. So a pound coin is never simply British currency; it also represents power or the lack of it. Similarly, hands are not simply the means by which we signal our handling of the material world; they are also indicative of how we form society and express some of the most important dimensions of our inner selves.

As we take the responsibility for ourselves into our own hands, the challenges of taking a stand for truth, for human dignity, and the just stewardship of the earth's resources begin to confront us. But the complexity of our lives as individuals and within the relationships and society we build will always call for the skill of handling failure, pain and costly reconciliation.

In all these respects we have said nothing that need be regarded as distinctively Christian. And yet this outline of the experience of being human is the raw material from which Christian revelation is drawn. It is in the givenness of our human capacities that God plants the means by which we sense God's presence and learn the habits of seeking to live within it.

Our exploration of what we are like has begun to suggest to us some of the ways in which we are capable of being like God, capable of 'kindness', as Janet Martin Soskice suggested. Being the same 'kind' as God is demonstrated as our hands reveal God's creativity in us, as they make present through symbolic means the reality of what is not seen or heard, and define through body language relationship space that cannot be measured.

We began this chapter with a reference to hands and sight. A concluding image returns us to that theme.

On the organ screen of Llandaff Cathedral there is a huge figure of Christ in majesty by the Jewish artist Jacob Epstein. Its location in the Cathedral was part of the post-war reconstruction after bomb damage. Epstein, whose personal life was at least as complex as that of Stanley Spencer, was reputedly conflicted about the task of marking the hands and feet of Christ with the wounds of the nails that are characteristic of the risen body. And the reasons for that conflict within him would be obvious, in the wake of the Holocaust and its roots in an anti-Semitism that had blamed the Jews for the death of Jesus.

But Epstein was not the first to hesitate to put out his hand towards the body of the risen Christ. The first person was Thomas the twin, who insisted that he had to use his hand to see if what the other disciples said about the resurrection was true. Thomas was taken to the brink when confronted by the sight of Jesus; at the point where time and eternity collided, he hesitated. Thomas had wanted to stretch out his hand to touch the resurrection, to see if it was real. That very human instinct is so profoundly symbolic of our age and the nagging doubt it has about faith and religion: is it for real?

Hands function symbolically in the Christian tradition as the means by which we articulate the reality of what is not seen. This may sound like an extravagant claim, but the prosaic routines by which the unseen reality is gradually understood are by no means arcane or elaborate. Those routines are called liturgy, which means 'public work'. They have at their core the simple tasks of bathing a child (baptism) and preparing and eating a meal (the Eucharist), although both liturgical works are always more than what they seem.

If thus far we have begun to perceive that in doing such things our hands can reveal more than we know, then we are ready to move on to consider the next stage of our exploration, the exercise of our minds in pursuit of what our hands reveal. We shall also, perhaps, appreciate the wisdom and beauty of Alice Oswald's poem, that captures in few words what I have struggled to say in many more.

> Here I work in the hollow of God's hand
> with Time bent round into my reach. I touch
> the circle of the earth, I throw and catch
> the sun and moon by turns into my mind.
> I sense the length of it from end to end,
> I sway me gently in my flesh and each
> point of the process changes as I watch;
> the flowers come, the rains follow the wind.
> And all I ask is this – and you can see
> how far the soul, when it goes under flesh,
> is not a soul, is small and creaturish –
> that every day the sun comes silently
> to set my hands to work and that the moon
> turns and returns to meet me when it's done.[6]

1   Hall, L. (2008), *The Pitmen Painters*. London: Faber and Faber, pp. 28, 58, 71, 75.

2   Soskice, J. M. (2007), *The Kindness of God: Metaphor, Gender, and Religious Language*. Oxford University Press, p. 5.

3   Ibid., p. 25.

4   West, E. G. (1978), 'Literacy and the Industrial Revolution', *Economic History Review*, 31, (3), 10.

5   Dowling, M. B. (2006), *Clemency and Cruelty in the Roman World*. Ann Arbor, MI: University of Michigan Press. Examples of these sarcophagi can be seen in the Museo Nazionale, Rome, the Uffizi, Florence, the Louvre, Paris, and the Los Angeles County Museum.

6   Oswald, A. (1996), *The Thing in the Gap-Stone Stile*. London: Faber, p. 40.

Chapter 2

Knowledge and Nostalgia

Place the helmet of salvation on my head, O Lord, that I may subdue devilish assaults.

A poster that was frequently seen in student rooms and houses when I was at university showed someone slumped in a hammock and a caption beneath it that read: 'Sometimes I sit and think, and sometimes I just sit.' This described all too adequately the mood of those times in my student career that were the day after the night before, when nothing much seemed to happen in one's mind until well into the afternoon.

I'm sure that students work much harder now, but I wonder about the provision made for learning how to handle the pressure of work and the demands of modern life. From an early age attainment targets seem to drive the educational agenda. Where do you go to escape?

A friend of mine who has a relentlessly busy job tells me that when life is too much, and sometimes even when it isn't, she goes to live in a parallel universe, somewhere in her mind. 'No, it's fine,' she says firmly, 'they know me there.'

A sense of access to another world is nothing new. The English composer William Byrd, writing in the late sixteenth and early seventeenth centuries, set to music a poem by Sir Edward Dyer that celebrates recourse to this place of escape:

> My mind to me a kingdom is;
> Such perfect joys therein I find.
> It far excels all worldly bliss,
> That world affords or grows by kind.

We observed in the last chapter that our hands can reveal to us more than we know. They also open up to us territory that invites further exploration, as the artist discovers on the canvas (or the pavement), the sculptor in working with clay, the bride and groom joining hands in wedlock, or the person who 'speaks' in sign language.

In a similar way, the mind opens up a 'kingdom' in which knowledge, memory and mystery are to be found. If we choose to embark upon an exploration of this new territory, it will reveal to us something important about ourselves. It will show that we exist not simply as a collection of functions, but as an organic unity that is beautifully and bafflingly complex, delicate and needy.

In this chapter we shall look in more detail at this mysterious thing that we call our mind, something that is intimately connected with our understanding of selfhood. We shall explore the sense of purpose and destiny that comes from being made by God and makes us restless, as St Augustine puts it, for our maker.

The Integrity of the Human Person

In the perception and practice of the Christian faith, the human person is a unity. It is not the hands alone, nor the head alone that inspire us or enable us to communicate. Integrity, that statement of being together, being whole, is about the nature of the integration of all that we are, everything about us that contributes to the ways in which we know and handle our experience of the world, other people, ourselves and God.

A deficiency in one of these areas of knowledge will have consequences that impair our capacity to know the others. So to live a life that is entirely self-absorbed will distort our ability to appreciate other people. To live in a world without God can skew our attitude to creation and to the potential of human life. And to explore these areas of life with only one part of ourselves will similarly distort our understanding of them. Our knowledge of God must engage body, mind and all that we are. It is also vital that we should take note of what contemporary scientific research has to tell us about the mind and how it functions as part of our being human.

In a recent Boyle Lecture in the Church of St Mary-le-Bow in the City of London, Malcolm Jeeves, an eminent Professor of Psychology, spoke about how to understand the relationship between psychological and neurological enquiry (research on how the brain works), and religion. Some areas of common ground emerged quite swiftly. One was that Christian faith is not dependent upon a belief that human beings have an immortal soul that is an added extra to the physical human body, or that the mind is an abstract, invisible thing. The unity of ourselves is intrinsic to the Christian understanding about creation and our relationship with God; this need not be in conflict with modern science.

The relationship between God and the human person is something that Professor Jeeves recognized as important for the perspectives of psychology and anthropology and their understanding of a human being. So when the Psalmist asks, 'What is a human being?' it is always in the context of the relationship with God: 'What is man that thou art mindful of him?' (Psalm 8.4) Our enquiry about human beings is not about a slab of flesh; it is about an organism that gains its meaning from its relationships. For the Christian, the relationship that determines our meaning is our relationship with God. This is the relationship that indicates what is eternal, not simply flesh alone. And it is a Jewish physician, Jeremy Goopman, who states that our relationship with God, with the eternal, is not 'a proper subject for study in the world of science'.

Fashions change in scientific disciplines as in any other. Where once it was only possible for scientific psychologists to speak of behaviour, now it is possible for them to enquire again about what we mean by mind. Here also Professor Jeeves offered wise counsel against the reduction of faith to neurological function. The suggestion, for example, that 'all persons who have religious experiences are having microseizures of the [brain's] right temporal lobe' needs to be treated with extreme caution as a scientific proposition. The evidence would seem to be more complex and less than reliable.

For Christians, and indeed all people of faith, there is good reason to regard scientists as people who are at least as capable of contributing to our understanding of faith, as they are of seeking to undermine

it. The benefits of the contribution of science to faith in God might
well outweigh any damage for which it could be used. Christians
ought therefore to be confident about the scope of scientific research
as something that can contribute positively to our exploration of the
mind as a territory of mystery. Here is an example from Professor
Jeeves' lecture of how this might be so.

In 2007 the Wellcome Foundation funded research into what part
of the brain responds to beauty. The leader of this project, Professor
Semir Zeki, maintained that the outcome of the exploration would
not damage the objective beauty of Michelangelo's *Pietà*. Whichever
part of our brain we use to appreciate the beauty of this work of art,
the appreciation still leads us to something greater: a sense of wonder.
So the understanding of how we respond to it with a function in our
brain is only one element in the phenomenon of what makes beauty.
Professor Jeeves' point is that in this instance, as in so many others
when dealing with the brain, 'more than one level of explanation is
necessary to do full justice to a phenomenon'.

One of the things I found most encouraging about this Boyle
Lecture was a renewed sense of confidence in the Christian tradition of the Scriptures that narrates the truth as scientists are now
interpreting it to us. This is especially true of the Psalms, a reposi-
tory of wisdom from which the Church draws daily in the Offices
of Morning and Evening Prayer. An example of this ancient wisdom, newly recognized again in scientific research, is in the 'mas-
sive amount of cognitive neuroscience work on face perception'
and the recognition of a relationship between a person's face and
trustworthiness.

In the ancient Jewish tradition the face of God was both a source
of blessing and the goal of all striving. So the blessing that God com-
manded Aaron to give to the Israelites in Numbers 6.25 is:

> The Lord bless you and keep you;
> the Lord make his face to shine upon you, and be gracious to
>   you;
> the Lord lift up the light of his countenance upon you, and give
>   you peace.

And in the Psalms, the quest for the face of God is synonymous with the pilgrimage of our life and all its vicissitudes:

> My heart hath talked of thee, Seek ye my face: Thy face, Lord, will I seek. (Psalm 27.8)
> When thou openest thy hand they are filled with good.
> When thou hidest thy face they are troubled. (Psalm 104.28–29)

Also associated with this sense of the blessing of the face of God is its guarantee as the trustworthiness of God:

> Offer the sacrifice of righteousness: and put your trust in the Lord.
> There be many that say: Who will shew us any good?
> Lord, lift thou up: the light of thy countenance upon us. (Psalm 4.5–7)

The general thrust of Professor Jeeves' lecture was towards a sense of integration between religion and science. He also pointed us towards an understanding of the wholeness of the human person as something to which both religion and science direct us. Another Biblical expression of this integration of ourselves is in its understanding of the process of ageing. The sign of God's blessing of Job, after all his afflictions, was that Job 'lived one hundred and forty years, and saw his children, and his children's children, four generations. And Job died, old and full of years.' (Job 42.16–17) Job's old age was a sign of blessing because it was also characterized by the wisdom that came from adversity and faithfulness to his God.

Lines of Communication

Growing old is something that today we are often encouraged to believe is a matter for regret, particularly in our appearance. But actually there is great dignity in ageing well, and in fitting with comfort and grace how you live with your memory and experience in the condition of your age. In the lined and crumpled face of W. H. Auden it was possible to read the signs of a life that intertwined many forms of abuse with longing, vision and beauty; it was exemplified by restlessness. Auden was never apologetic for how his face got to be the way it was. In another face, similarly lined, that of Mother Teresa of Calcutta, one saw a different kind of strain, but longing, vision and beauty were also integral to the relentlessness with which she drove herself to encounter Jesus in the world's poor.

In both instances we see a physical, facial indication of something beyond the material framework of human life, as Professor Jeeves suggested in his Boyle Lecture. For both Auden and Mother Teresa faith was, in very different ways, a means by which the immaterial was apprehended. The restlessness of their quest for that immaterial reality, God, told in the lines on their faces.

Auden identified the poet's recognition of faith in the healing and freedom that exist within the confines of space and time:

> In the deserts of the heart
> Let the healing fountain start,
> In the prison of his days
> Teach the free man how to praise.

These are words that he wrote in February 1939, in memory of W. B. Yeats, who had died the previous month. In Auden's tribute to Yeats, one poet recognizes in the work of another a voice that answers the call of memory and longing. This is where the experience of life demands meaning and might discover it through faith. The statement of what has happened to us is not a sufficient account of what we need to say; events point us beyond themselves and ask us for an exploration of why they matter. This is not a comfortable exploration of learning and discovery.

The joyful stringency of religious life lived by Mother Teresa was her response to a world so bent on self-destruction that it wounded her perception of humanity as something beautiful, made and loved by God. A different kind of woundedness is seen in Auden's own attachment to lacerating relationships. They were 'hideously entangled, yet he longs for the simple certainties'; this was the verdict of one friend and supporter towards the end of his life. It matters not that much of this laceration was self-inflicted; it enabled Auden to appreciate humanity and the poetry of Yeats, who had experienced similarly inspirational wounding in Ireland. As Auden notes:

> Mad Ireland hurt you into poetry.
> Now Ireland has her madness and her weather still,
> For poetry makes nothing happen: it survives
> In the valley of its own making where executives
> Would never want to tamper.[1]

Poetry's survival solely 'in the valley of its own making' is perhaps too pessimistic an assessment of the effect of poetry and the scope of its impact upon us. For although poetry 'makes nothing happen' to the material world, it can powerfully shape our apprehension of creation – the earth, other people, ourselves – and of God in ways that expand our vision and deepen our understanding. Poetry can be the articulation of meaning in which we locate our faith. Its capacity to bend language to meaning that is beyond the normal patterns of discourse makes it well suited to the task of speaking of God.

Weather and location as the raw material of poetry can powerfully evoke aspects of life that are beyond our material sphere of reference and open up the possibility of faith. The American poet Robert Frost belonged to the same generation as Auden's father and was an acquaintance of Yeats, though he never cared for Auden. However, Frost covers similar territory to Auden in his poem 'Desert Places', in seeing that we have it in us to find a world beyond this one.

> Snow falling and night falling fast, oh, fast
> In a field I looked into going past,
> And the ground almost covered smooth in snow,
> But a few weeds and stubble showing last.
>
> The woods around it have it – it is theirs.
> All animals are smothered in their lairs.

I am too absent-spirited to count;
The loneliness includes me unawares.

And lonely as it is, that loneliness
Will be more lonely ere it will be less –
A blanker whiteness of benighted snow
With no expression, nothing to express.

They cannot scare me with their empty spaces
Between stars – on stars where no human race is.
I have it in me so much nearer home
To scare myself with my own desert places.[2]

Here the themes of weather and location convey a sense of nostalgia for something lost. The expectation of life being 'more lonely ere it will be less' hints at this, as does the reference to 'my own desert places'. The details of Frost's life suggest where this sense of desert loss might originate. In 1900 his first child, Elliott, died, aged four. In 1934, two years before the publication of 'Desert Places', Marjorie, his youngest daughter and his favourite, died, aged 29. His life would be seared by further tragedy. In 1938 his wife Elinor also died and his son Carol committed suicide two years later. But the loss of these people he has loved is also a prelude to some sense of the recovery of them, when loneliness 'will be less'.

A sense of loneliness and emptiness in the landscape that Frost finds in his mind is articulated by the Jesuit Karl Rahner, in his *Encounters with Silence*, written in a prose style that acts as though it were wanting to be poetry. In the chapter entitled 'God of the Living' Rahner writes about the dead he has known and loved. He imagines them as part of a procession, 'and this column grows ever shorter and more quiet, until one day I myself will have to break off from the line of march and leave without a word or wave of farewell, never more to return'.

There is something very matter-of-fact about this description. But it is also an expression of love, in the recognition that a unique place is occupied in Rahner's life by those he has loved: 'there is no substi-

tute for them; there are no others who can fill the vacancy when one
of those whom I have really loved suddenly and unexpectedly departs
and is with me no more'.

In his address to the God of the living, Rahner is articulating a
prayer that is an expression of the human emotion of nostalgia. It is
far from being the mawkish, introspective indulgence that can sometimes be mistaken for this strong but tender human emotion. Like
other emotions, nostalgia can be a means by which we intensify the
mind's focus of prayer.

Death stirs a yearning in our minds for what we have: life with
those we love; and for what we have never seen or known: that life,
but beyond death. (Let us acknowledge this, mindful of the verdict of
Professor Jeeves we have recently noted: more than one level of explanation is necessary to do full justice to a phenomenon. Death may
not be the only reason for this yearning.) This yearning concentrates
our attention on the God for whom all men and women are alive,
and so, on the God in whom ultimately all our longing is vested.

This is the God who holds our memory as our future, the God
who knows us in the mind that is our kingdom, as Edward Dyer put
it. What Rahner is wrestling with in his mind is the silence of that
place to which his dead have gone, and the silence of God as the one
in whom they rest. This is like the silence evoked by Robert Frost
in the image of 'A blanker whiteness of benighted snow/With no
expression, nothing to express'.

How do the lines of communication work here? When someone
who has been a part of ourselves is no longer there, like a limb ampu-
tated by death, how does that visceral sense of their remaining presence work? You open a door and expect her to be sitting there. You
see a film, hear news of a friend, or visit a grandchild and think that
you must remember to tell the person you always tell, but you cannot; he is dead. It's Christmas and you want to buy her a present to
say, 'You are still real to me.' Our dead are silent and yet the tug of
their lives pulls our minds towards them in the familiar expectation
of a response.

To describe these lines of communication as nostalgia is by no
means intended to trivialize them. It locates them in the working of

our minds that yearns for what has been part of us. But from the experience of a yearning such as this we can discover an understanding for what we have not yet been able even to imagine – a kind of borrowed nostalgia. It is to a description of that borrowing that we should turn.

We began this chapter on the mind with a consideration of the drift of science and what it teaches us about the integrity of the human person. Professor Jeeves gave us good reason to be confident that science need not undermine the Christian experience of trust in God, whose face we seek. We have seen in the faces of two very different people, W. H. Auden and Mother Teresa, the physical signs of a spiritual yearning. This yearning echoed in the poetry of W. B. Yeats and Robert Frost, in both instances arising out of a wound from which they drew the haunting beauty of their poetry. At this point poetry met prayer in the reflections of Karl Rahner.

Let us now look more closely at what contribution nostalgia makes to the phenomenon of the yearning of our minds for the knowledge of God.

A Borrowed Nostalgia

Nostalgia, in its richest, most abundant sense, is one way of describing our wistful imagining of our silent dead. But how does this nostalgia connect with the human longing to understand the love of God? At what point does it tackle the pain of grief and the evil of death?

Confronted with the relentless silence of our dead, we require something like a sign language to interpret their resting in the God for whom all men and women are alive. This is a point at which we have become the people without hearing, while they, our dead, are those who will hear the songs of heaven. We can no longer see them, though they, we believe, will see the vision of God. The signs, symbols, language and ritual of Christian faith and worship are our instruments for accomplishing this interpretation. That is why poetry, art and music, the oblique sciences in the narrative of faith, are indispensable for our demonstration of how we cross the barriers between sound and silence, between sight and its loss ('a blanker whiteness of benighted snow'), between time and eternity.

The nature of the realm from which the love of God crosses into ours begins to become apparent with Rahner's description of his dead as imitating the silence of God, which is 'the earthly manifestation of the eternal word of [God's] love'.[3] What does he mean by that?

The impression that things are reversed when we cross from earth to heaven, from time to eternity, is something that features as a consistent observation in the Christian experience of God. It is like a theological magnetic north. This is an extension of much that we hear in the gospels stated with disarming simplicity: the first shall be last, and the last first; the hungry are fed with good things, the rich are left empty; prostitutes and tax collectors go into heaven ahead of the guardians of religious rectitude, and so on. So here, silence on earth is the true medium for the intimation of heavenly sound. In similar ways that we shall explore in later chapters, others will intuit darkness as the medium for the revelation of divine light, or white, dazzling light for the outbreak of the beauty of colour in the manifestation of the glory of God.

So it is in silence that those whom we have loved and recognized in their voices, among other ways, remain hidden from us but alive in the mind of God, to whom Rahner's prayer is addressed:

the words of their love no longer reach my ears, because they are conjoined with the jubilant song of Your endless Love . . . My dead live the unhampered and limitless Life that you live . . . and thus their life and their love no longer fit into the frail and narrow frame of my present existence.

Nostalgia is associated with all manner of senses – sound, smell, taste and vision. It is also closely associated with a sense of place and time. These are associations that we have already noted in Robert Frost's poem. But there is also an understanding within the Christian tradition that we can borrow our sense of nostalgia. This becomes possible when we allow the tradition to shape and inform the story of our present identity.

One example of this is the belief that we are, as Genesis tells us, exiles from Eden, that paradisal place where we walked with God as friends and lived in complete harmony with our environment and each other:

> O unexpected stroke, worse than of Death!
> Must I leave thee, Paradise? Thus leave
> Thee, native soil, these happy walks and shades
> Fit haunt of Gods?

This is the way Milton describes the trauma in Book XI of *Paradise Lost*.[4] But Milton is standing here in an ancient tradition. So when Thomas Aquinas writes a hymn in honour of the work of our redemption by the Word of God, Jesus Christ, the final petition of the hymn is for our return to Eden, the place of our creating, the metaphor for heaven:

> O grant us life that shall not end
> In our true native land, with thee.

Eden is not the only place that expresses our nostalgia for a return to where we experience friendship with God. Jerusalem is also firmly in the Christian mindset as identified with that friendship and unity: 'Jerusalem is built as a city: that is at unity in itself. For thither the tribes go up, even the tribes of the Lord: to testify unto Israel, to give thanks unto the Name of the Lord.' (Psalm 122.2–3) The nostalgia for Jerusalem, as for Eden, is identified with a vision that is of the past and the future. This is because in the Christian Apocalypse, the Revelation of John, the new Jerusalem, the heavenly City, takes to itself the qualities of Eden, in the river that flows from it and the tree of life that grows within it.

But there is another experience of exile that informs this metaphor about Jerusalem: the exile of the people of Israel in Babylon. There, in a foreign land, sunk in shame and confusion, they are fearful that God has abandoned them. They live in separation from the Temple, where God was present. And the Temple is itself desecrated by those who do not appreciate its power and holiness. This is an experience that gives rise to one of the most haunting expressions of nostalgia in the Old Testament, Psalm 137:

> By the waters of Babylon we sat down and wept: when we
>   remembered thee, O Sion.
> As for our harps, we hanged them up: upon the trees that are
>   therein.
> For they that led us away captive required of us then a song and
>   melody, in our heaviness: Sing us one of the songs of Sion.
> How shall we sing the Lord's song: in a strange land?

One of the beautiful Christian hymns that alludes to this borrowed nostalgia for a place we never knew but is part of our history, is written by the twelfth-century theologian and philosopher Peter Abelard. A man of amazing brilliance, he will always be remembered for the turmoil and beauty of his illicit and doomed love affair with Héloïse, the niece of a Canon of Notre-Dame in Paris. Héloïse eventually became an Abbess at Ferreux-Quincey, near Troyes, where Abelard had founded the Oratory of the Paraclete. It was for Héloïse and her sisters that Abelard wrote a collection of hymns, of which the best known is possibly 'O quanta qualia sunt illa sabbata' ('O what their joys and their glory must be, those endless Sabbaths the blessed ones see' in the translation by the nineteenth-century Anglican priest J. M. Neale).

This hymn was intended to be sung at vespers on Saturday evening. It is part of the prelude to Sunday, the day of resurrection on which the Church celebrates the realization of our risen life with God in the heavenly Jerusalem:

> Truly Jerusalem name we that shore,
> 'Vision of peace' that brings joy evermore!
> Wish and fulfilment can severed be ne'er,
> Nor the thing prayed for come short of the prayer.

It is neither sentimental nor unrealistic to discern here a mood of nostalgia. The obvious goal of our longing is Jerusalem, a theme that Abelard returns to in a subsequent verse:

Now in the meanwhile, with hearts raised on high,
We for that country must yearn and must sigh,
Seeking Jerusalem, dear native land,
Through our long exile in Babylon's strand.

Our knowledge of Abelard's love for Héloïse, the subject of a
remarkably beautiful novel by Helen Waddell, is one reason why we
might find him so poignant a hymn writer. There is infinite tender-
ness and a refreshing absence of contemporary moral judgement in
Waddell's telling of the story in novel form, just beneath the surface
of which lie contemporary accounts from Abelard and Héloïse themselves. 'The pleasures of lovers which we shared have been too sweet
– they can never displease me, and can scarcely be banished from my
thoughts,' writes Héloïse in one of her letters.

In some respects we are back with Stanley Spencer and his image of
Jesus holding the scorpion. There is pain in the relationship between
Abelard and Héloïse, certainly, but also the strength of an incredibly
tender love. Although for Spencer the pain of his own marital situation was largely psychological, for Abelard it was both psychological
and physical: he was castrated as a punishment for his love of Héloïse
and they suffered the pain of exile from each other for the rest of
their lives.

In both stories the experience of human love does more than
simply inform the mind in recollection; it also functions as a metaphor or stimulus that prompts desire for God. 'Wish and fulfilment
can severed be ne'er . . . we for that . . . must yearn and must sigh.'
These words, intentionally sacred, might also have their origin in the
human experience of physical love, the more so since the imposition
of physical separation did not, as Héloïse indicates, banish her recollection of their love.

For Abelard and Héloïse nostalgia for Jerusalem was itself a profound narrative of their longing for each other. In the hymn it
becomes also a paradigm of their longing for God. (It could equally
be the case that their longing for God was a paradigm of their longing for each other.) The appearance at the end of time of the heavenly
City adorned as a bride for marriage would also be the fulfilment of

their nostalgia for the consummation of their love. There human love would be perfected, made eternal in being conjoined with the jubilant song of God's endless love, as Rahner described it.

This reference to being conjoined with a jubilant song is an allusion to one of my favourite hymns. It was written by St Bernard of Cluny, an exact contemporary of Abelard and Héloïse, and describes the heavenly Jerusalem as being 'conjubilant with song'. The hymn is a gorgeous paean of longing for something that is not yet known – a borrowed nostalgia. But the longing is also for something that is essentially social. The City is thickly peopled with figures who sing and shout in celebration, and yet, writes Bernard, 'I know not, O I know not, What social joys are there, What radiancy of glory, what light beyond compare'. Here we borrow from the best experiences of our social life on earth a sense of what we might be longing for in heaven, nostalgia for what we've not yet begun even to imagine.

Our survey of the kingdom of the mind has so far concentrated mainly on the personal dimensions of nostalgia. But in a borrowed nostalgia the character of life for which our longing is nurtured is invariably social. In this longing the relationship of two must be complemented by more than two in order to be itself, to be fulfilled. It cannot sustain the potential for exclusivity in mutual admiration. Nor is three a description of limitation; it is a symbolic number for God who is without limit.

The social dimensions of this longing will take us to a consideration of the nature of our relationship with the three persons of the Trinitarian God, and a return to how science encourages our articulation of faith as social – always more than two. But we begin with an episode at the end of Helen Waddell's novel that points to the wider, social significance of life and redemption in heaven.

'You'll Never Walk Alone'

After being hideously punished by her uncle for his love for Héloïse, Abelard returns to teaching and Héloïse is forced into a convent where she becomes the Prioress. The novelist in Helen Waddell writes up the involvement of Thibault, a mutual friend of the separated lovers who is able to give them news of each other. One evening Thibault and Abelard are chatting when they hear a thin cry of intolerable anguish; it is a rabbit caught in a trap, but Abelard fears it might be a child.

The uncertainty of who or what is caught in the trap leads to a discussion about the existence of suffering in creation. The rabbit that Abelard rescues from the trap dies in his arms. Although he admits that his own physical suffering was justly deserved, Abelard's compassion for the dead rabbit prompts him to wonder about all innocent suffering: ' "Then, Thibault," he said slowly, "you think that all this," he looked down at the little quiet body in his arms, "all the pain of the world was Christ's cross?" '[5]

The suffering of the rabbit is significant, even though it is not human suffering, and the reference to a 'little quiet body' strengthens the allusion to childhood. This is a highly effective way of exploring in our minds things that are true about ourselves and about what we have made of the world. By removing the exploration and admission of the truth to a distant time, sufficiently remote from our adult life, we can often discuss serious aspects of our life quite openly. It is easier, for example, to ask a group of adults to admit to one thing in childhood of which they are ashamed, than to ask for a description of something similar from within the last month or the last year.

The disjunction between our adult selves and our childhood selves can serve to allow us freedom to explore our minds in challenging and perhaps uncomfortable ways. It is also characteristic of us as adults that we can identify with children as though they were our other selves, the small, vulnerable people that we still are within. For this reason the scandalously low importance we attach to how children are treated in our society is perhaps an indication of something dysfunctional about how we actually view ourselves.[6] If children can become a commodity, a love object to be indulged or exploited for the love we expect from them in return, then it is almost certain that we are making a serious statement about the status and impoverished quality of our own lives. Relationships are then sought for the sake of what they can do for me and not for their own sake as a statement of mutual enrichment.

It was within a society tearing itself apart because of its extremes of poverty and wealth that the Russian novelist Fyodor Dostoevsky wrote, in *The Brothers Karamazov*, his most devastating account of human suffering. He focuses particularly on the suffering of children as a challenge to a neat account of forgiveness and harmony.

The challenge is issued in an emotional outpouring by Ivan to his younger, other-worldly brother, Alyosha Karamazov. Having reviewed the catalogue of torments done to children, Ivan concludes that a ticket for access to harmony at the end of time, through the forgiveness of their tormentors in heaven, or at the expense of envisaging hell, is simply not acceptable. 'It is not God that I do not accept,' says Ivan, 'I merely respectfully return him the ticket.' And in response to Alyosha's accusation that this is rebellion, Ivan replies, 'Rebellion? I'm sorry to hear you say that . . . One can't go on living in a state of rebellion, and I want to live.'[7]

The debate between Ivan and Alyosha about children, suffering and redemption needs to be placed in the wider context of Dostoevsky's novel, which is the death (or is it murder?) of their father. This tumultuous event, if it was murder, is a metaphor for the elimination of God from the realm of human thought or consciousness. Ivan is in some respects making the case for why this might be unavoidable: God has to take the ultimate responsibility for allowing the suffering of children. Their suffering is a fact, and nothing that he can see, neither forgiveness, nor punishment, can make it better.

Thibault, in response to Abelard's comment that all the pain of the world was Christ's cross, attempts to take that observation further. 'God's cross,' he says. What he means by this is that God the Father also bears the suffering of the cross. It is a proposal that might appear to meet the objections that Ivan raises in Dostoevsky's novel, by suggesting that God takes to Godself the inflicting and the suffering of pain and thereby somehow gets a lever on how it might be redeemed.

It is a view that the German theologian Jürgen Moltmann has articulated in his book *The Crucified God*, where he responds to Ivan's challenge. Moltmann suggests that the cross of Jesus should be understood 'as death in God', that is to say that it is a death experienced within the life of the three persons of the Trinity: 'Christ hanging on the cross [is] the "outstretched" God of the Trinity.' This does not mean that God dies, but that 'the history of God contains within itself the whole abyss of godforsakenness, absolute death'.[8]

The idea that God has a history is not, of course, to be taken literally, as though a biography of God could be written down. But the phrase does have some merit in helping us to think of what there is in God in ways that are analogous to what exists within our own minds. It prompts us to think about what it means to be human, to live in society. It asks us to attend to Ivan's comment that he cannot go on in a state of rebellion; he wants to live.

We should return at this point to Professor Jeeves' Boyle Lecture. There we find an important affirmation of the significance of the social as the context in which the existence of religion is to be understood. He maintains that on the basis of scientific evidence it would be simplistic to identify religious words and behaviour with any particular structure and functions in our brain. The psychological and sociological evidence that makes sense of religion also provides an affirmation of religion's essential, theological nature. It is an enterprise of faith to which science might lead us, but is unable to carry across the boundary of knowledge into experience. That bit we have to leap across ourselves.

The nature of religion's theological identity is social; it requires us to take the doctrine of the Church seriously, to understand ourselves corporately, as a people. Professor Jeeves reminds us that it is with all the saints – the whole people of God – that we can comprehend 'what is the breadth and length and height and depth, and . . . be filled with all the fullness of God' (Ephesians 3.18–19). This understanding is not the agglomeration of individual impressions triggered in our brains. How might we account for this scientifically?

The reference to all the saints is not simply a pious one. It is derived from an analysis of football as a phenomenon that could not be produced from the way people are individually 'hard-wired' in their brains. Football, for players and spectators, cannot emerge from a particular kind of neurological function; it is the product of skills and organizational capacities that exist for a wide variety of reasons and are practised in many different aspects of our life.[9] And if we are right to understand that the very nature of religion is to be located in how we function together as human beings, this points us to a serious breaking down of the idea that my mind is my kingdom where I and God meet alone. By a cheerful coincidence, the great song of the Liverpool football terraces is a perfect summing up of this truth: 'You'll never walk alone'.

The proposition 'God is' commits me to the recognition of others as the foundation on which that very realization of faith is itself built. This is why Ivan Karamazov is in agony. The torments of children and animals are connected with his life, are in his mind even though he was not the perpetrator or victim of them. His life, like ours, our destiny, and therefore the possibility of faith in God, are all intertwined. But what Ivan has not fathomed is the extent to which the history of God contains within itself the 'whole abyss of godforsakenness, absolute death', as Moltmann puts it.

We draw this chapter on mind to a close with a final section on what it might mean to say that godforsakenness and absolute death are in the mind of God. They are there because we are there, resting in the death that is distinctively our contribution to the sheer pity and sadness of things. But they are not hidden in God in the way that we hide nuclear waste in the bottom of the ocean, where it remains sealed and inert in its destructive contamination. Our deadness is the material from which redemption is made. It is the waste of our lives that is worked upon by the creativity of love in order to reveal new beauty that is not subject to the death from which it was made.

What might we say about the process of this redemption? How might we think of Ivan as being capable of receiving it? Could we imagine anyone persuading him to end his rebellion and live?

The Might of thy Great Loving

Ivan Karamazov is a very modern person. He represents our penchant for contractual relationships and for protest when those contracts do not suit our book. In *The Brothers Karamazov* he is given the most powerful lines, but shares with his younger brother the struggle of faith and doubt. Alyosha's struggle is driven, in large measure, by his encounter with the Elder Zossima, a figure modelled on St Seraphim of Zarov.

St Seraphim exemplifies the charism of transfiguration, a sign of holiness characteristic of the Eastern tradition of Christianity. This is a state of being clothed with the divine light. Its counterpart in the Western tradition is stigmatization, being marked by the wounds of Christ, as was the case with St Frances of Assisi and St Catherine of Siena. With both transfiguration and stigmatization the mind's perception of an intense identification with Jesus expresses itself in bodily manifestation. It is an example of what we have been calling the integrity of the human person, a statement of how longing and fulfilment cohere within me, so that I can anticipate what I shall be, my borrowed nostalgia, in the reality of my present existence.

This integrity is displayed in an account by a young man named Nicholas Motovilov of his meeting with St Seraphim in 1831. Motovilov described the Staretz, the Holy Man, as an authentic bearer of the Holy Spirit. In their meeting, St Seraphim becomes a crucible of heavenly fire. His words to Motovilov indicate the authentic nature of the gift of the Holy Spirit as contagious, expansive and profoundly joyful. Motovilov can hardly bear to look at the Staretz because light is flashing from his eyes and he is dazzled by the brightness of the old man's face. But St Seraphim instructs him that he too is shining with the fullness of the Holy Spirit, otherwise they would not be able to see each other.

The description of the transfiguration in which they both participate is worth quoting in full:

> Then I looked at the Staretz and was panic-stricken. Picture, in the sun's orb, in the most dazzling brightness of its noon-day shining, the face of a man who is talking to you. You see his lips moving, the expression in his eyes, you hear his voice, you feel his arms around your shoulders, and yet you see neither his arms, nor his body, nor his face, you lose all sense of yourself, you can see only the blinding light which spreads everywhere, lighting up the layer of snow covering the glade and igniting the flakes that are falling on us both like white powder.

This description of transfiguration has many of the hallmarks of a resurrection appearance about it. Three emotions seize Motovilov: peace, joy and love. These are the themes that Jesus outlines to his disciples in the intimate moments of their conversation before he is arrested, tried and put to death.

In that highly charged atmosphere of final instructions and leave-taking, Jesus bequeaths to his disciples a hold on these three gifts through the sending of the Holy Spirit, to which St Seraphim attributes the grace of the experience of transfiguration. Here is the kingdom that is the mind of Christ. By the power of the Holy Spirit it also becomes characteristic of our minds, a dimension of the divine and the eternal within us that we have yet to become capable of knowing in its fullness.

St Seraphim's closing instruction to Motovilov turns to this theme of the kingdom and our participation in it:

> This kingdom is just the grace of the Holy Spirit, living in us, warming us, enlightening us, filling the air with his scent . . . The Lord seeks hearts overflowing with love for him and their neighbour . . . 'Give me your heart', he says (Prov. 23.26). For in the heart he builds the kingdom of God.[10]

'Give me your heart' is a powerful statement. It sums up for us the way we think of everything that we are. We envisage the heart as the seat of our emotions, but the gift of it is also the action of the will, of the mind. What does it mean for us to give our heart?

We sing about it, at the end of Christina Rossetti's carol 'In the bleak midwinter': 'but what I can, I give him – give my heart'. The disturbing quality of this carol is often lost in the sentimentality that overtakes Christmas. But for nineteenth-century England it held a subversive quality: in the realism of her reference to 'a breast full of milk', in her Tractarian theology that refers to Mary's 'maiden bliss' (for some, this came close to Roman Catholic piety expressed in the immaculate conception), and in her reputation for an association with the erotic in her poetry.

Realism about our embodied selves, the divine love that makes, chooses and delights in us, and the fruitful use of our affective capacities – all these might well be starting points for a description about what it means to give your heart. But this is a request, perhaps above any other, that can never be theoretical. Nor can it ever be simply an individual thing. In order to undertake this amazing act of loving wilfulness, we have to be asked by another person, or to be so bold as to do the asking ourselves. From every which way, it is an issue of love.

What emerges from the transfiguration experience in Motovilov's account of St Seraphim is an amazing sense of the simplicity of the request. It is something that Rossetti also captures. We spend much of our lives calculating risks, doubting the worth of daring to commit, anxious about its cost. And because of the dislocated nature of our nurture at school, at home or among friends, many of us lack opportunity to rehearse or witness the social grace that makes this moment a familiar possibility in which we dare to say, simply, 'Give me your heart', or if asked, we dare to give it.

Not long ago I came across an account of a mother and daughter shopping in Oxford. A group of musicians were busking in an open space and people stood around listening. Mum and daughter joined them. Delighted by the music and the atmosphere of the small crowd the daughter stepped forward and began to dance. Her enthusiasm overcame her and she started to invite others to dance, taking them by the hand to entice them into her world of delight in music and the freedom it released. People started to move away, embarrassed. Eventually her mother put down the shopping and stepped forward, took up her daughter's hand and danced. Her daughter was a teenager and had Down's Syndrome.

Writing about this episode the girl's mother explained how she had also been self-conscious and embarrassed. But there was something so utterly irresistible in her daughter's request that she overcame her fears. It had been a simple request, and it was not difficult to say yes. 'Give me your heart' was what her daughter had asked, and in return she would give delight and freedom, life in its fullness.

We referred earlier to music as one of the oblique sciences of the narrative of faith. I do not believe it is far-fetched to connect the music that inspired the young daughter out shopping in Oxford, with the halls of Sion that are conjubilant with song. In her mind music spoke about something that transcended the limitations of our earthbound, image-conscious society. To my mind she stands at the conclusion of this chapter as an angelic figure. I do not mean by that something sentimental or dressed in tinsel wings. Angels are not that; they are messengers who disturb our minds with the interruption of heaven.

If there were a messenger who could disturb the rebellion of Ivan, she would be that angel. And music could indeed be the oblique science that her often oblique mind might choose to accomplish it. 'Give me your heart' she would say as she invited him to live. It would be the moment of his redemption.

The idea that love can redeem through itself, without reference to contract or ticket, is pervasive in Christianity. Such a view lends itself, unsurprisingly, to song in hymnody:

> Free us from sin by might of thy great loving,
> Cleanse thou the sordid, loose the fettered spirit,
> Spare every sinner, raise with thine own right hand
> All who are fallen.[11]

In this chapter we have attempted to survey what our minds might hold. We had already discovered that our hands could be capable of symbolizing a reality beyond themselves, revealing more than we know. The scientific enquiry into the working of our minds has revealed amazing facts about the structure and function of our brains, but it also hit boundaries it could not cross. Science alone cannot account for beauty or for the faith that is the corporate identity of a people, the Church. So in a way that is similar to our discovery about hands, we find that our minds, beginning with something material, open up to us the reality of something immaterial: a kingdom, in the opinion of Sir Edward Dyer, and of the Staretz St Seraphim.

Nostalgia for that kingdom is witnessed too in many ways, the lines on aged faces being one eloquent example. This nostalgia is also a yearning for the redemption of humanity; it is social as much as it is about the transformation of my own experience by the joy of love. This transformation may be experienced between lovers (Abelard and Héloïse), or it may flow from an altogether more theological and discursive source (Karl Rahner or Jürgen Moltmann). However is it received, this joyful love is the fruit and gift of the Holy Spirit, the constant breaking out of the Holy Trinity from two into three.

But it is from the hands of the teenage daughter in the centre of Oxford that we take our cue to move to the next chapter, on clothing. She has shown us what might pierce the rebellious heart of the modern atheist. As one of those whose cause Ivan had championed, she asks him, 'Give me your heart', and so demonstrates that only love can liberate us from rebellion. Our next chapter looks at how love is communicated.

1   Mendelson, E. (ed.) (1976), *W. H. Auden: Collected Poems*. London: Faber, pp. 197–198.
2   Barlow, A. (ed.) (1998), *Robert Frost: Selected Poems*. Oxford University Press, p. 48.
3   Rahner, K. (1960), *Encounters with Silence*. London: Burns & Oates, pp. 54, 57.
4   Lines 268–271.
5   Waddell, H. (1987), *Peter Abelard*. London: Constable, p. 201.
6   A UNICEF report on the well-being of children in twenty-one industrialized countries, published in February 2007, placed Britain bottom of the list.
7   Dostoevsky, F. (1978), *The Brothers Karamazov*. Harmondsworth: Penguin, (vol. 1), p. 287.
8   Moltmann, J. (1974), The Crucified God. London: SCM Press, pp. 207, 246.
9   The analysis was originally with baseball, and the reference is Brown, W. S. (2006), 'The Brain, Religion, and Baseball: Comments on the Potential for a Neurology of Religion and Religious Experience', in McNamara, P. (ed.), *Where God and Science Meet. Volume Two: The Neurology of Religious Experience*. Westport, CT: Praeger.
10   Zander, V. (1975), *St Seraphim of Zarov*. London: SPCK, pp. 91–93.
11   Ante-Tridentine Breviary, translated by Alan McDougal.

Chapter 3

Power Dressing

O Lord . . . may I, with those who have made their robes white in the blood of the Lamb, enjoy the delights of eternity.

I am not an early morning person, and never have been. Getting dressed can consequently be a bit of a challenge. In fact, I am beginning to get the hang of the morning stuff, and getting dressed is less of a problem these days. In part this is helped by being a priest. It minimizes the decisions about what to wear. As long as it's black, it will do for me and the simple addition of a clerical collar avoids all that stuff with choosing a tie.

Perhaps there is more than a streak of laziness here, in a lack of willingness to make bold decisions in the light of a new day. I can't help feeling, though, that some people's bold decisions are a bit of a challenge to the rest of us when revealed in public. The livid green tie has its place, but probably not with that shirt. The scale of the chrysanthemums in the print on that dress might just possibly be accentuating an area that could do with less attention being drawn to it, but I could be wrong.

Standing in the Marks and Spencer's queue to pay for my milk and morning paper, I become aware that other people have done much more than me in choosing how to get dressed courageously, imaginatively, provocatively, expensively and suitably.

The process of getting dressed raises important questions for us about fashion and how it influences us. Perhaps getting dressed is one of the moments in the day when we have to confront ourselves and ask who this person is that I am preparing to present to the world. How we dress is an unavoidable expression of that person. Will our

manner of dress reveal or disguise what we see within? At one level
the process of dressing is a superficial one, but at another level it also
connects with the issues of what we have been and how we are fashioning our lives now.

In thought, idiom and culture there seems to be an irresistible
link between fashion and God. It is partly to do with a sense of our
identity as creature and God as creator, but we express it in ways
that do not at first appear to be remotely connected with any serious theological viewpoint. What follows may seem an odd way to
proceed, but let's be a bit James Bond for a moment, to show what
I mean.

It is a hot evening; the scene is a glittering party in Cannes. Someone amazing arrives; heads turn, this glorious creature captures everyone's attention, and Sean Connery steps forward: 'You look divine; and
I adore leopard skin.' They sweep into the hotel ballroom together.
Cut. End of scene.

Of course in the context of a James Bond film we wouldn't take
this frivolous and superficial comment seriously. But having recognized that getting dressed raises questions, albeit fleetingly, about our
identity and creatureliness, we might legitimately enquire about the
association of ideas it prompts in the mind of 007. Trivial charm
thoughtlessly uses language for God and worship to express itself. At
an uncalculated level, something much deeper than cocktail party
pretence is surfacing.

The profound importance of fashioning and re-fashioning things
for glory and worship is what lies at the heart of the Bible. In this
chapter we look at some of the ways in which that surfaces in our
experience of life and in our attitude towards God, one another and
the earth.

We begin with an exploration of language, and an observation of
how fashion and worship are connected. What emerges from this is a
sense of the seriousness of what we can easily take for granted. That
seriousness often only emerges from the experience of misuse, which
is what idolatry does to worship. We then consider how God re-
works the patterns of misuse to achieve perfection and beauty. This is
God's fashion: that nothing be lost, and all shall be well.

Fashion and Worship

As a noun, the word fashion is a thermometer of modern life and a significant factor that determines what we wear. However, as a verb this word is closely, but not exclusively, associated in the English language with the action of God, whom we often describe as fashioning things. In the Old Testament we use the word fashion to translate three Hebrew words that mean to form, to prepare and to do. In the Psalms and in the book of Job a refrain echoes from that distant time, saying to God, 'Thy hands have made me and fashioned me.'

The resonance of that echo is caught in a more contemporary tone by Gerard Manley Hopkins. Here the formation of new words mirrors the fashioning by God of things in creation, as Hopkins seeks to make his language reflect the delicate force of nature's vitality.

> Delightfully the bright wind boisterous ropes, wrestles, beats
>   earth bare
> Of yestertempest's creases; in pool and rut peel parches
> Squandering ooze to squeezed dough, crust, dust; stanches,
>   starches
> Squadroned masks and manmarks treadmire toil there
> Footfretted in it. Million fuelèd, nature's bonfire burns on.

Having given this amazingly fluid expression to the power of nature, and noted the 'manmarks' on it, Hopkins then goes on to describe the human person as nature's 'clearest-selvèd spark' whom 'death blots black out'. But God's fashioning of the human race is, by God, redeemed in Christ:

> since he was what I am, and
> This Jack, joke, poor potsherd, patch, matchwood, immortal
>   diamond,
> Is immortal diamond.[1]

This vision of redemption as the outcome of God's fashioning in creation is also the echo of an earlier articulation, in this case by St

Paul. The term to fashion is again used in the English translation to identify the purposes of God in the work of Christ. In the letter to the Philippians the Authorized Version of the Bible reads that Jesus will 'change our vile body, that it may be fashioned like unto his glorious body' (Philippians 3.21). The strength of language to describe our natural condition would be offensively unappealing but for the fact that it provided Evelyn Waugh with the title of a good novel, Vile Bodies – an ironic reference to privileged life in Mayfair in the late 1920s. Waugh's association of this term with a satire on fashion and decadence might just rescue it from the danger of being used to reinforce patterns of self-hatred that we shall note later in this chapter.

As far as St Paul was concerned the activity of fashioning is also profoundly intriguing. It is about the creative power of God that is evident in the life and work of Jesus Christ. However, there is another Biblical use of the term to fashion where the outcome is not life but extinction in the form of death. In the book of Exodus there is an account of Moses going onto the mountain to speak with God during the pilgrimage of the children of Israel from Egypt to the promised land. Moses is on the mountain for forty days and nights and, as we noted in Chapter 1, this is when the finger of God writes on the tablets of stone the ten commandments.

During that time the people get restless, thinking that Moses has abandoned them, and they ask Aaron for gods who will lead them. Aaron collects together the people's gold, plunder that God had instructed them to take from Egypt, and 'fashioned it with a graving tool' into a golden calf (Exodus 32.4).

What is significant about the fashioning of the golden calf? The answer is perhaps most clearly stated in Psalm 106, which also describes the same episode:

> They made a calf at Horeb: and worshipped the molten image.
> Thus they turned their glory into the similitude of a calf that
>   eateth hay.

Aaron, the priest of God fashions something from his own imagining that represents the people's desire and it becomes the object of their worship. It distorts the delight of the people, skewing their attention from God their creator and sustainer, to whom alone worship is right and proper.

In the Christian tradition we believe that worship gives glory to God. The connection between glory and worship is underlined in Psalm 3, verse 3, where early translations into English of the Hebrew text use the words worship and glory interchangeably: 'But thou, O Lord, art my defender: thou art my worship (glory), and the lifter up of my head.'

Worship also has an effect upon those who offer it, whatever the object of their worship might be. The worship of God re-forms, or re-fashions: we are changed and our worth is expanded as we grow in the experience of those things that are the nature of God in Godself. These are things such as the love, delight and unity of relationship, as revealed in the three persons of the Trinity; the ability to appreciate and sustain the beauty of creation; the desire to re-create what is wasted by misuse. The Anglican spiritual writer Evelyn Underhill describes the worship of God in these terms:

> Worship is the great spiritual action of mankind . . . It is the homage paid by the soul to its origin . . . [it] is our contribution to the purpose of the universe . . . We can only know in a real sense that which we love, gaze at, and enjoy, and this is worship.

In worship we also give to God what God has not given to us: the wonder and recognition of God's worth. Underhill's descriptions of worship all underline the importance of human action in worship as something that dignifies being human. It is 'great spiritual action' and not insignificant, because in it we play a part in God's purposes for the universe achieving their ends. But this action can only be properly transformative as an expression of our love and wonder freely given.

Worship is not a form of divine taxation; the duty of worship lies in delight, its obligation arises out of the desire to do it. The re-fashioning of us that it brings about is stated with eloquent poise in the Eucharistic rite of the Book of Common Prayer: 'And although we be unworthy, through our manifold sins, to offer unto Thee any sacrifice, yet we beseech Thee to accept this our bounden duty and service; not weighing our merits but pardoning our offences.'

Acceptance is the fashion statement here. But it is a dynamic statement, not a static one. We don't ask for a label that suggests completion; we seek a lifestyle that strives to shape and model a way of living that characterizes the gospel values of Jesus Christ. We wish to be made nothing less than acceptable in heaven.

From our contemporary use of the word acceptance we have a good sense of what it might mean as a description of social, relational status and recognition. So we might comment that someone finds acceptance at work rather difficult because of his dress sense. Or we might observe that 'in spite of prejudice, her tenacity and mental acuity won her acceptance as a leading defence lawyer'. Acceptance in these instances is about how we fit all of who we, our lifestyle and values, are into a particular context.

Acceptance, or its absence, rejection, is one of the driving forces of today's Western culture, fuelled in large part by the fashion industry. We are terrified of being ourselves. We are afraid that the unique contribution we have to make to the diversity of human life and experience will not conform to standards that others set as fashionable, though they might well be standards that do not fit our unique identity, price range, or the shape we have become.

By contrast, worship begins with the acceptance of our frailty, oddness and limitation ('although we be unworthy, through our manifold sins'). From this it moves to the recognition that even in this condition we can be accepted ('not weighing our sins but pardoning our offences'), because that is the dignity of being able to worship.

This phrase 'pardoning our offences' hardly does justice in English to the ancient Latin text it translates. The Latin words are *veniae largitor*, which literally mean a giver of forgiveness. But the word *largitor*, giver, is cast in the direction of liberal generosity. It has the overtone of recklessness, a giver who is heading towards being a spendthrift, giving away all there is to give. That generosity is the condition from which our acceptance by God flows; it is what characterizes the divine fashioning of us.

Heaven is what we are about in worship rightly orientated towards God. If our worship is accepted, it fits with the ceaseless hymnody of the cherubim and seraphim: it is fit for heavenly and eternal purpose. As a result we regain the dignity of paradise in being connected with something beyond the limits of this world that is subject to decay and death.

This contrasts starkly with the worship of what we ourselves have fashioned. That worship turns our attention back on ourselves and away from God, who made the fashioning possible. The point is not that human artistry and skill are in any sense flawed. Evelyn Underhill, again, recognizes that 'the inspiration of the painter, the musician, and the poet, and often that of the scientist and explorer too, contains a genuine element of worship'.[2] But misdirected worship that puts us in the place of God leads to a profound damage of human dignity and relationships; it also alienates us from the earth and its life-sustaining systems.

At this point we should turn to the question of taking fashion seriously. As the French social theorist Roland Barthes noted, 'Fashion is both too frivolous and too serious at the same time.' Our James Bond throwaway line about fashion, 'You look divine; and I adore leopard skin' is a piece of nonsense that we should also deal with seriously. There is something subtler about fashion and self-worth, about being 'divine', that we must explore first. It begins to identify the power of worship, and the importance therefore of understanding what it is we worship, why, and what that worship does to us.

In the habitual routine of getting dressed, the clothes we wear can make statements about what we adore or what we despise – what it is we really worship. What are the consequences of worshipping our own ideals, our own fashions? We look first at an example of how the damaging misuse of worship can be restored and then in the final section of this chapter we look at the place of loveliness and delight as fashion statements about human dignity and the Christian vocation.

Fashion and Idolatry

The origins of our tendency towards idolatry, the misuse of worship, are located in the book Genesis. Here the storyline is again about the misuse of freewill, the worship of novelty and the attraction of what is superfluous. All of these things are present when, in the midst of plenty, Adam and Eve choose to eat the apple. They do it because they can. Not because they have to, or because it will bring any necessary benefit; simply because they have been told they can. It's a reason we still buy stuff today. There are two small details in this narrative from Genesis that are important for our consideration of fashion.

The first is when Adam and Eve realize that they are naked. This is the moment, according to the story, that registers some terrible interruption in the relationships between human beings and with God. Shame, the fruit of deceit, overwhelms them and as the history of humanity's neurosis with itself begins, 'they sewed fig leaves together and made loincloths for themselves' (Genesis 3.7).

Another consequence of Adam and Eve's misuse is that they are exiled from paradise, where they had walked with God as friends. (We alluded to the borrowed nostalgia for this place in the previous chapter.) Work, pain and contention are the future destiny of the humankind that God has made to enjoy freedom and dignity. But they do not leave paradise without signs of God's care for them: 'the Lord God made garments of skins for the man and for his wife, and clothed them' (Genesis 3.21).

The reformer Martin Luther described the transformation of the dignity of Adam and Eve as a change in the fashion of their lives, the loss of their glory, which had been unimpeded communication with God – worship in its perfected form. They are no longer fashioned as God intended, but as they have made themselves. The Latin phrase Luther uses to describe the new, fallen humanity is *incurvatus in se*, turned in upon oneself.

This captures very well what we have been saying about the distortion of worship. The symbol of our inability to walk upright with God in friendship, as in Eden, is the fact that we are, by nature, habit and fashion, turned in upon ourselves. In these circumstances it becomes all too easy for us to worship what we have made, because the fashion of the human race has become stooped, curved in self-regard.

In the grounds of Chester Cathedral there is a wonderfully imaginative sculpture by Stephen Broadbent that is a meditation on this theme of being curved in upon oneself. It illustrates the story in John's gospel of the Samaritan woman at the well. She gives Jesus a hard time when he asks her for a drink of water and, reading between the lines, we get the impression that she is a bit of a handful. But the rapid exchange between her and Jesus unlocks her brittle defences, reveals her shame, and allows Jesus to dispel it by the taste of participation in the worship of heaven.

Stephen Broadbent's sculpture rolls Jesus and the Samaritan woman into a circle. Jesus forms the lower part of the circle, sitting upright. The woman is curved round and looks down into his upturned face. Broadbent captures the intimacy and force of the story, and the quality of worship that is integral to it. This is what Underhill describes as a capacity to look into the eyes of God, and to love and gaze and enjoy.

In Broadbent's sculpture the woman's introspective gaze has been interrupted by Jesus, who has, as it were, got down underneath her shame and caught her eye in order to lift her vision and begin to stand her upright before God and the society in which she was living. What was the cause of the shame? Its existence is clear from the fact that she lies to Jesus about her situation.

The woman has had five husbands and is presently living with a man she is not married to. There is something here that she has fashioned in her life of which she is very ashamed. Another important element in the story is the woman's social exclusion. She is at the well alone in the heat of the day because she does not want to incur the disparaging and judgemental looks of others; that only accentuates her shame and loss of self-esteem.

It could be unwise for us to speculate too much on what the woman's story is, or to make judgements about her. But the evidence that John gives us suggests a person who has loved much, as another story puts it. For what reasons might this woman have said of a former husband, 'I worshipped him, but . . .'? We do not know, but in contemporary Britain we could complete her sentence in a number of ways that would explain her situation: '. . . but he was violent'; '. . . but he was having an affair'; '. . . but he abused my children'.

What we see in her we all too often see in ourselves: the tragedy of the destructive worship of an ideal embarked upon in sincerity and hope. This is what Exodus and the prophets mean by idolatry: it is the worship of something or someone who does not have the means to sustain what it takes to be the object of worship, which is the ability to give and sustain life. Idolatry of a particular kind has led this woman, if not to extinction, then to exclusion, and the terrible pain of a person curved in on herself in fear and resistance to the scorn of other people. It is a situation that Jesus meets with immense patience and compassion. How will it be resolved?

Right at the end of their encounter the Samaritan woman is still baiting Jesus, answering him back from the store of her own knowledge. He talks about worship, and she virtually interrupts to say, 'I know all about that Messiah stuff': ' "When he comes, he will proclaim all things to us." Jesus said to her, "I am he, the one who is speaking to you." '

In the Greek text of the story, what Jesus actually says is, 'I am, the one who is speaking to you.' It is a dangerous answer, because among the Jews 'I am' is the name for God that is never spoken by mortals, and here Jesus is using it of himself. This is the point at which the sculpture unlocks the mystery of true worship as transformative and healing. Getting beneath her defences and bravado, Jesus finally looks into her eyes, and reveals himself as the God who made her and fashioned her, in our English parlance. At last she is silent, and that's the moment the sculpture captures, when she looks at Jesus and becomes capable of worshipping the person who will give her life. But that's not the end.

The presentation of Jesus in this story as weary and sitting on the ground, has been read elsewhere, in the requiem hymn, the *Dies Irae* (Day of Wrath and doom impending), as a statement of identification with the labour of the cross:

> Quaerens me sedisti lassus,
> Redemisti, crucem passus,
> Tantus labor non sit casus.

Faint and weary thou has sought me,
On the Cross of suffering bought me;
Shall such grace be vainly brought me.

Again, this English translation doesn't quite capture the subtlety of the first line in the Latin text, where the word *sedisti* alludes specifically to Jesus sitting down in weariness, as he does at the well. But when we read the verse of this hymn back into the Broadbent sculpture and conclude the story of the passion with the resurrection, as we must, the re-fashioning of the woman at the well becomes clear. When Jesus stands, rising from the dead, so the circle he has entered to engage with those curved in upon themselves is reshaped. As Jesus gets up, so he uncurves the Samaritan woman's perspective, restores her to dignity and will ultimately stand her on her own two feet as a statement of new dignity and confidence.

At the end of John's account of this incident the Samaritan woman is indeed on her feet. She has become an evangelist, telling the people of Sychar, her town, 'He told me everything I have ever done.' She became the witness to her social, psychological and spiritual healing and it brought the townsfolk to find Jesus and ultimately to believe in him.

The fundamental issue for the Samaritan woman is that she is freed from the tyranny of introspection. No longer is she committed to anxiety about her motives, loves and objects of adoration. There is someone else who knows her through and through, and can direct her attention to a horizon beyond herself; herein she finds her liberation.

This is part of what caused the conversion of St Paul and of one of the towering intellects of the early Church, St Augustine. In both instances there was release from the worship of their own ideals. In Paul's case he was a fanatical agent for the implementation of the Jewish law; in Augustine's case the intelligent reasoning of his own mind was in danger of confining him within the categories of a philosophy that could have obscured the possibility of faith in Jesus Christ.

In our own day the fashion of sustaining ourselves at the centre of our worldview is a burden of responsibility for the world that is beyond our competence or capacity. We cannot stop famine, war, injustice, greed or global warming, simply by legislation, and though we can limit its effects, we often choose not to. The fate of the Millennium Development Goals will be our generation's judgement in this regard. The burden of thinking we can save the world and ourselves is something from which we often seek release.

This does not mean that we are to give up hope and the struggle of engagement with the forces of resistance in this world. It does mean that we are delighted to find something, someone who can bear this burden, who can sustain the earth, our life, our minds, and liberate us to be responsibly dependent, instead of being independently dominant. We discover that we do flourish when we express our responsible dependency in the worship of the God who made and fashioned us.

We have been using the term fashion in a very technical, Biblical sense. We have seen that it is closely associated with worship, because, fashioned by God, we recover our perspective when we turn our gaze towards our creator. But we have also seen that the worship of what we ourselves have made is characteristic of a curving in upon ourselves that can have damaging consequences. The most serious of them is the loss of our knowledge of God's unconditional love for us.

W. B. Yeats recognized this with touching insight when he wrote this poem for Anne Gregory. Like Anne, we might seek to fashion ourselves in ways that will make us the object of other people's attention (worship). But the searing honesty of who we really are is something that only God can love, for only God can see and bring about perfect beauty from our imperfections.

> Never shall a young man
> Thrown into despair
> By those great honey-coloured
> Ramparts at your ear,
> Love you for yourself alone
> And not your yellow hair.

But I can get a hair dye
And set such colour there,
Brown or black or carrot,
That young men in despair
May love me for myself alone
And not my yellow hair.

I heard an old religious man
But yester night declare
That he had found a text to prove
That only God, my dear,
Could love you for yourself alone,
And not your yellow hair.[3]

The extent to which we fashion ourselves or other people into an image of our own ideal or their ideal is what we have been considering in this section on worship and idolatry. The question to which we now turn is how the damage of our pursuit of fashion as idolatry can be re-fashioned into new beauty.

Much of our attention has been on distortion and damage. But the Christian hope is relentlessly committed to the experience of delight in the life that God has given us: 'Love to the loveless shown, that they might lovely be', in the words of Samuel Crossman's seventeenth-century hymn. The emphasis here should be on the quality of God's love for us, that we might lovely be. Issues of image, self-worth, death and extinction are all pertinent to this question of the healing that frees us to delight in loveliness. As we turn to the final section of this chapter on fashion and clothing, we seek an affirmation of the attainment of that loveliness.

Fashion Victims

A recent poll among teachers revealed that children who cannot afford fashion clothing and kit are often isolated or bullied at school. The general secretary of the Association of Teachers and Lecturers,

Dr Mary Bousted, commented that 'Children feel under immense pressure to look right and having the right brands is part of that.'

This is an example of insidiously damaging misdirected worship. The brand is of our own making and need not be evidence of design or artistic merit (think of football shirts); it invites 'adoration', another description from marketing; it promises to fashion the wearers or users into some kind of status they do not presently have; it results in discrimination, possibly violent, against those without this brand, especially if the reason is that they are too poor; the guarantee that its manufacture has not exploited the poor or the earth's resources (in either production or distribution) has rarely been part of its appeal; the brand's benefits are ultimately financial for those who produce and sell the branded item.

These are all major considerations in the factors used to influence the way we dress, and the kit we use. When children are already subject to intimidation and bullying in the face of these influences, we should not add to the pressures on them by imposing an adult expectation that they withstand peer-group pressure. We adults don't show many signs of doing so with much confidence, and the economics and advertising of fashion, the forces that create that pressure, are largely of our making.

But children are not the only fashion victims. Another example of fashion damage that affects people of all ages is an anxiety about our shape and size, though the seeds of this anxiety can be sewn in childhood. Dr Susie Orbach's influential book *Fat is a Feminist Issue* is a powerful statement about the expectations imposed on women to conform to a certain shape in order to be regarded as 'divine'. And why should one shape be more 'divine' than another?

David Brown makes the point in his book *God and Grace of Body* that our idea of what makes a body 'divine' is culturally determined: 'in the seventeenth century fat was seen as a sign of prosperity (and thus of health) and so was integrated into contemporary perceptions of what it was to be beautiful'.[4] The damage that the transient idols of fashion might cause can be life threatening, in the case of an eating disorder, and life-long, in cases of irreparable damage to self-esteem in formative years.

For those who are victims of bullying, or struggling with anxiety about size and diet, the desire to be accepted and to be lovely is really important. But this is also true for us all. When we get dressed we ought properly to want to make a statement about our self-worth and to present ourselves as persons in whom care is taken of what God has fashioned. We should want it for other people as much for ourselves, because we believe that life should be vital, edgy, unpredictable, worth living, and self-presentation is an element in the affirmation of life's richness. That's partly why people love a good James Bond film.

What is the Christian contribution to this sense of the goodness, worth and vitality in life? What role does clothing play in our articulation of it? To begin our answer we should return to the two references in Genesis about sewing fig leaves together and God clothing Adam and Eve with skins. We are dealing here with two distinct forms of clothing, one of human, the other of divine making. What is the significance of this?

Let's begin with the divine one. The author in Genesis does not say what the skins are that the Lord God uses for making these clothes. It seems improbable to suggest that God had hunted and killed animals, skinned them and made them into clothes. The misuse of leopard skin, for example, for this purpose would seem to contradict the very nature of the relationships between creator, humankind and the animal kingdom that constitute the life of paradise. So are these skins some kind of symbol? This clothing represents the compassion of God for the human race, and within the clothing itself lies the pledge of future restoration. They do seem to have a symbolic quality. What might it be symbolic of?

Elsewhere in *God and Grace of Body* David Brown reminds us that in Michelangelo's fresco of the *Last Judgement* on the wall of the Sistine Chapel, the apostle St Bartholomew holds his skin in his hand (he was, by tradition, martyred by being flayed alive). The face in the skin is a self-portrait by Michelangelo. Brown sees this as indicative of the artist's interest in what reveals inner and outer beauty. In this case the skin becomes the symbol of a human life, St Bartholomew's, lived in heroic discipleship of Jesus Christ, through which an eternal destiny is revealed. As further explanation of the identification between artist and saint Brown quotes a line from what might be Michelangelo's last poem: 'My dear Lord, you who alone clothe and strip me'.[5]

Our skin is a good symbol of our lives. In childhood we see gentleness and vulnerability; we also see amazing capacity for growth, transformation and rapid healing. As we grow into our skin, as our individual character appears and we take our place in society, the colour of our skin can become something that is profoundly important when it marks us out as different from others. We can be judged by our skin. We can allow those judgements to diminish us, or we can struggle to find beauty in our skin, because we know it is God's gift to us.

As we grow old, our skin begins to tell the story of how we lived our lives. We commented on this earlier with reference to the 'lines of communication' in the faces of Mother Teresa and W. H. Auden. But there will be other stories recorded in our skin. The scars left by operations, accidents or violence done to us will be evident. So too will the ways in which we have chosen to mark our skin, for pleasure, beauty or shame with piercings and tattoos. There may also be other marks on us that are the silent, anguished cries for help, or evidence of a destructive addiction.

The story of pregnancy and childbirth will also be there, as will the signs of rituals that mark cultural ritual and initiation. The story of our love will also be recorded, not only in the lines of laughter or grief, but through a ring worn so long on a finger that its mark is indelibly part of us. And if all of this is the story written in our skin, then it makes perfect sense to imagine that the clothing of skin that the Lord God gives to Adam and Eve was simply loaned until the day God would be seen in it himself in order to lead us back into the relationship and paradise from which we had exiled ourselves.

The image of God being clothed in our flesh is characteristic of the way many of the early Christian writers describe the incarnation. Among my favourite descriptions is one that is read just before the beginning of Advent and the preparations to celebrate the birth of God in our flesh, or our skin as we are suggesting here:

Christ, the heavenly king and the true husbandman, came to humanity laid waste by sin, he clothed himself in a body and carried the cross as his implement and cultivated the deserted soul. He pulled up the thorns and thistles of evil spirits and tore up the weeds of sin. With fire he burned up all the harvest of its sins. When thus he had tilled the ground of the soul with the wooden plough of his cross, he planted in it a lovely garden of the Spirit; a garden which brings forth for God as its master the sweetest and most delightful fruits of every sort.[6]

The telling of a story through the skin or the flesh as a form of clothing may sound somewhat gory to our clinical age, but it continues to attract artistic interest. In 2006 Damien Hirst's 35-foot-tall statue, entitled *Virgin Mother*, was shown in London as part of the Summer Exhibition at the Royal Academy in London. It reveals a heavily pregnant woman, striding forward on her plinth. One side of her is covered with skin, the other side is not, revealing her skull, sinews, muscles and the child in her womb. It is a disturbing sight. But it is also inescapably a picture of ourselves at some point in our lives, as child or parent.

For our purposes, the significance of the statue lies in the skin. On the side that has skin we see an incredibly beautiful woman. In the momentum of her pilgrimage her head is raised so that she walks with dignity, but also as a person who is captivated by some vision beyond our sight. She is the confident, liberated antithesis of the human condition of being turned in upon ourselves. But what of the skin?

It could appear that the skin taken from the Virgin Mother to reveal the inner workings of our biological identity is the skin that the Lord God has taken to wearing within her womb. This is the skin that will clothe God, the second person of the Trinity. It will still tell a story like ours. The lines of laughter and grief will be there, as will the signs of strain and toil.

In this skin God makes the racial history of a woman and her husband God's own and so redeems it. The details of that history illuminate our understanding of God's plan for the human race from the moment that Adam and Eve left Eden. It is a plan for recovery of dignity and a return to friendship with God.

Just as we can trace our own story in the skin that is ours, so the evangelist Matthew traces an ancestry that delineates the story Jesus inherits in his skin (Matthew 1:1–16). It is important to understand the extent to which that story embraces all aspects of being human. Those details are part of the skin in which God lives on earth, to bring us back to paradise, to heaven. But the way back may well be complex and unpredictable. A poem simply entitled 'Tamar' captures the scope of this:

> Exceedingly odd
> Is the means by which God
> Has provided our path to the heavenly shore:
> Of the girls from whose line
> The true light was to shine
> There was one an adulteress, one was a whore.

> There was Tamar who bore –
> What we all should deplore –
> A fine pair of twins to her father-in-law;
> And Rahab the harlot,
> Her sins were as scarlet,
> As the thread which she hung from the door.

> Yet alone of her nation
> She came to Salvation
> And lived to be mother of Boaz of yore.
> And he married Ruth,
> A gentile uncouth
> In a manner quite counter to Biblical lore;
> And from her did spring
> Blessed David the King,
> Who walked on his palace one evening, and saw
> The wife of Uriah,
> From whom he did sire
> A baby that died – oh and princes a score.

And a mother unmarried
It was, too, that carried
God's Son, who was laid in a cradle of straw,
That the moral might wait
At the heavenly gate
While the sinners and publicans go in before,
Who have not earned their place,
But received it by grace
And have found them a righteousness not of the Law.[7]

Whatever we are like, exceeding oddness is God's chosen way of getting the human race to the heavenly gate. The poem suggests that no oddness is outside the scope of the compassion of God. Nor is it simply oddness of shape or appearance. The complexities of our love and the response it finds in others is also enfolded in this dispensation. Adherence to the changing laws of fashion does not earn us entry, nor does adherence to any other law that does not convey grace – a word that simply means gift.

As we seek to live in our skin with all its inherited character and the contribution we have added to its shape and appearance, the question of what it means to be lovely, with the seriousness envisaged by Samuel Crossman, still confronts us. This is where fashion and clothing meet resurrection.

Artists who have tackled the task of portraying the resurrection have to address the question of clothing. The gospels are silent on the matter of the clothing of the risen Jesus, except that John states that the grave clothes were left in the tomb. Michelangelo makes the bold decision to sculpt the risen Jesus without any clothing other than the skin of his risen body. In doing so, he is connecting with a tradition, contemporary with the time of Jesus, that depicted the ancient gods as naked. The application of this convention to worldly authority and power, bestowing divine status upon an earthly emperor, is something that the British Museum's 2008 exhibition of the life of the Roman Emperor Hadrian demonstrated most effectively.

Michelangelo's statue of the risen Jesus is in the church of Santa

Maria sopra Minerva in Rome and has, for most of its history, been supplemented by a variety of loincloths. Jesus stands holding the instruments of his death that become the signs of our redemption; they are the cross and rope that bound him to it, and the pole and sponge on which he was given vinegar to drink. A subtler reading of the sculpture sees that the binding to the cross and the clothing in skin are similar statements of God's identification with humanity. Torture and fashion form an interesting statement of the human condition!

The challenge of the nakedness of the risen Christ should not startle us, however. We have already noted that an Advent reading prepares us to take this stark manifestation of God in our skin seriously. So does the magnificent hymnody of Advent when it directs our adoration to the resurrection body:

> Those dear tokens of his passion
> Still his dazzling body bears,
> Cause of endless exultation
> To his ransomed worshippers:
>   With what rapture
> Gaze we on those glorious scars!

Charles Wesley's hymn identifies the history of the incarnate life of God, including all its torture and death as the sign of glory. Here we properly worship because our gaze is turned from ourselves to God's transformation of ourselves in Jesus, who is fully human and fully God. The hymn identifies the hope that inspired St Paul to speak of the transformation of our body, 'that it may be fashioned like unto his glorious body'. That transformation is a part of our exultation in the glorious scars in the skin of the risen Christ.

Other gospel stories of the resurrection also focus on the body and confirm that the skin in which Jesus meets the disciples is the re-fashioning of the skin in which they had known him and witnessed his death. He shows them hands and feet and side as evidence. But in this new skin the things that previously had been closed to him are closed no longer.

Jesus enters a room in which the doors are locked. Here is a statement about what resurrection skin is like. The things denied us are now open to us. For some this will include mobility, sight, hearing and independence. It will also include social inclusion, inviolable dignity, freedom to love and ability to accept being loved. We have seen that what we worship has the capacity to affect us profoundly. So the worship of God in the risen, scarred, dazzling body of Jesus has the capacity to lift our vision to the transformation of our lives in the skin with which we are presently clothed. Worship of the risen Christ holds within it the celebration that we 'might lovely be'.

But we are also clothed in clothes, and in most presentations of the resurrection, so is Jesus. The clothing is simple, and it is generally white. This conforms to the accounts of the transfiguration of Jesus on the mountain prior to his arrest and death. That vision anticipates the resurrection. In the vision the clothes of Jesus are described as 'dazzling white, such as no one on earth could bleach them' (Mark 9.3).

Clothing features consistently in accounts of heaven in the Old Testament, as it does in accounts of resurrection life in heaven in the New Testament. White is the symbolic statement of such clothing, and it is used to describe the character of our being there. In the Revelation of John the great multitude from every nation, tribe and language that stand before the throne of God are 'robed in white' (Revelation 6.9).

We shall return to the significance of being robed and 'made white in the blood of the Lamb' when we come to the conclusion at the end of this book. But we conclude the final section of this chapter with a reference to the clothing also spoken of in Genesis. This was very home-spun, a new venture, made by Adam and Eve when they sewed fig leaves together.

One of the oldest sayings in the English language refers to an advance on Adam and Eve's first attempts at fashion and clothing with fig leaves. Eve developed the art of spinning, and presumably weaving, while Adam got on with the gardening, possibly growing plants that would be helpful to their fashion industry, like jute and hemp. Their cottage industry inspired the rebel priest John Ball to put the question during the Peasants' Revolt of 1381: 'When Adam delved and Eve span, where was then the pride of man?'

The point made by John Ball's question is one that sums up much of what we have been considering in this chapter. If clothing were value-free, a neutral commodity that was the same for everyone, how much less pride and idolatry there would be.

What we weave not only produces fabric from which a garment can be made; it also makes a statement about our identity, our engagement with the earth, and, today, our place in a global society. An example of this is to be found in Nepal, where in the Khosi hills in the eastern part of the country there is a long history of weaving a nettle fibre, known locally as allo. The fabric produced can be used to make sacks and bags, but it can also be treated to reveal a silken quality in a light fabric of great strength.

Weaving in this part of Nepal is not only a traditional art; it is also a source of income for some of the poorest people in that land, and a means of protecting the natural habitat. A link has been established between the nettle weaving area of Nepal and textile students from England who have gone to learn a lost art of making eco-friendly cloth and to contribute to making that cloth beautiful in ways that had previously not been envisaged. The main benefit in seeing the making of traditional items preserved and new skills developed lies in an improvement in the prosperity of this Nepalese community.

But there is also of benefit to us in the West. St Paul's Cathedral has recently been in a partnership with Central St Martins College of Art and Design in order to produce new vestments. We have been fortunate to work with some of the most gifted international students, who have designed amazing silks in brilliant colours, and used a mixture of contemporary and traditional forms of decoration to fashion the vestments. One of the award-winning graduates, Marie Brisou, completed a set of designs for St Paul's and left to go to Nepal. There she spent three months working alongside the nettle weavers, learning from them and contributing to their design skills.

When Marie returned from Nepal, she spoke with passion and conviction about the experience of living a very different life and learning much that we have forgotten about textiles. Her admiration for a culture in marked contrast to our own was, I thought, a real challenge to our world of fashion and its products. This is not because I think that silk, beautifully woven, is inherently bad. It isn't, and we use it unapologetically. But Marie's experience of textile production in Nepal was about giving and enhancing quality of life. By contrast, our fashion culture in the West is so often about inducing destructive anxiety about size, image and economic exclusion.

The capacity of fashion clothing to enhance the life and dignity of the disadvantaged and demoralized is not restricted to nettle weaving in Nepal. Milan, a major centre for the rag trade, sponsors an annual fashion show in its San Vittore prison for women. The women prisoners produce the clothes by hand and then model them. The transforming effect of beauty and recovered dignity is remarkable. Gabriella, who is serving a sentence for drug-dealing, comments, 'We have learned to make anything and everything . . . and you know it's giving you a future.'

The power of the loom, as a symbol of production by hand, is something that has engaged the imagination for as long as there has been story-telling. Penelope, waiting for the return of Odysseus, weaves all day, and undoes her work by night, in order to keep suitors at bay. She will not marry again until the tapestry is complete, and, of course, it never will be. It becomes the symbol of her fidelity and the unfolding of her life in grief and longing for her husband.

Similarly, a tradition recorded in the second-century *Book of James* describes Mary, the mother of Jesus, as a woman who spins and weaves to make the curtain of the Temple. Here again there is a deeper symbolism in the story. At the moment of the death of Jesus, the consummation of his mission, that curtain was torn in two from top to bottom. The rending was a sign of something momentous taking place. Mary's woven cloth provided a symbol for Jesus to use in the future accomplishment of his mission. It was, if you like, the equivalent of opening a book at a clean page, in order that a calligrapher could write in bold and glorious script the title of a new chapter in the history of human tragedy and redemption.

What will we do to unravel the loom of self-interest and our damage to earth and human life? We can accept the challenge to be different. A review of our wardrobe does not necessarily mean throwing it all out and starting again with allo fabric because that's now fashionable. Or we might actually decide that we really don't need more new clothes until the ones we've got really have worn out, no matter what they look like or how bored we have become with wearing them. Can we reconfigure our sense of beauty to discover it in generosity, kindness, laughter, spontaneity, and not in cosmetically produced surface attraction, or shiny clothing? Do we look good in clothes that have damaged the earth and screwed the lives of those who made them?

This is all too much to deal with first thing in the morning. But at some point during the day, during my life, I have to confront it, as a matter of urgency. Extinction may not threaten me quite yet; but I may be the cause of its threatening others today.

The final word on this subject of fashion and clothing goes to a Carmelite nun who understood true prayer and worship. She saw that we are living in an age that is losing the custom of those ways, as we become more fearful and absorbed in ourselves. But she had not lost hope:

We must try to understand the meaning of the age in which we are called to bear witness.

We must accept the fact that this is an age in which the cloth is being unwoven. It is therefore no good trying to patch. We must, rather, set up the loom on which coming generations may weave new cloth according to the pattern God provides.[8]

---

1   Gardner, W. H. (ed.) (1979), *Gerard Manley Hopkins: Poems and Prose*. Harmondsworth: Penguin, pp. 65–66.

2   Menzies, L. (1946), *Collected Papers of Evelyn Underhill*. London: Longmans, Green and Co., pp. 65, 66.

3   Albright, D. (1990), *W. B. Yeats: The Poems*. London: J. M. Dent & Sons Ltd., p. 295.

4   Brown, D. (2007), *God and Grace of Body: Sacrament in Ordinary*. Oxford University Press, p. 30.

5   Ibid., p. 212.

6   From the fourth–fifth-centuries collection of homilies attributed to St Macarius of Egypt.

7   Quoted by Bishop David Hope in a sermon; the author is not identified. Hope, D. (1993), *Living the Gospel*. London: Darton, Longman & Todd, pp. 11–12.

8   Mother Mary Clare, SLG (1988), *The Simplicity of Prayer*. Oxford: SLG Press.

Chapter 4

Binding Time

Bind me, O Lord, with the girdle of purity and extinguish disordered passion within me.

Years of driving a car taught me that it's possible to comment quite audibly about other people's driving, appearance and behaviour, and not be heard by them. I am now learning that a far higher degree of discretion is called for on a bicycle. This is especially true during the summer, when car windows are open. Drivers and pedestrians can hear quite clearly the observations one might make about their driving, appearance or behaviour. Mercifully, people on scooters and motorbikes can't.

This rule of self-awareness also applies to other contexts, as I learned some time ago on the River Wear, while still a student in Durham. Punting cheerfully upstream with friends, we passed several anglers sitting motionless on the riverbank. They were never pleased to see us heading into the quieter waters of their pastime, but bore our intrusion with glum and silent resignation as we narrowly avoided their lines, but successfully frightened away the fish.

From the other end of the punt the wife of a friend of mine commented loudly, as though we were in the privacy of a car, 'I really don't understand the attraction of sitting there all day long doing nothing.' I couldn't help feeling that sitting in a punt on the River Wear doing nothing much for a large part of the day didn't put us in a strong position to criticize the anglers. I'm also ashamed to admit that I did rather sympathize with her point of view. This left me somewhat handicapped in my ability to make any response in support of the excitements of angling. Instead, I smiled weakly, nodded conspiratorially to the anglers, and attempted what limited measures are possible in a punt to move swiftly on.

However, with the benefit of time, the error of my youthful view of angling has become clearer to me. Not that I have invested in rod and line and the other equipment and tackle needed to spend time in all weathers fishing on the riverbanks, but I have become theoretically fascinated by three aspects of this recreation: time, the line and silence.

In this chapter I want to use those three things to explore ways in which God binds Godself to us, and how we seek to respond to that commitment. The idea of being connected by a line, a thread, with the life of God is perhaps both a challenge and a comfort. This line is an expression of God's commitment to us in absolute and irrevocable self-binding. That may be a comfort; the challenge lies in asking how we should respond.

Commitment is something we find very difficult to handle. The two other dimensions, time and silence, are also challenges to us. We either have too little time or, in the extremity of the old age to which many of us now live, we have too much time and little capacity to do anything with it. Nor does silence come easily to us. We are accustomed to living with sounds that demand our constant attention; they have often become a substitute for human company, and without these sounds we feel very lonely.

Time is a fundamental part of the mystery of our relationship with God. When viewed from our own perspective, this is often stated as the difficulty of finding enough time in our busy lives to attend to the relationship. For some the difficulty is in finding time for church; for others it is in finding time to read, or to pray, or simply to reflect on what faith is. These are often the first casualties in the competing demands of a busy diary. I am by no means immune from failure in this regard, and the mere fact you are reading this suggests some level of success on your part.

It is very easy to beat ourselves up about not having time for God, but I'm never too sure whether we know what we would do with the time if we had it. I suspect that in a busy life of holding down a job and/or bringing up children, balancing the competing demands on our time means that what we need is a rhythm of contact with God. By this I mean regular, easily accessible moments and actions that turn our attention to God, and become the threads of eternity interwoven with the hours of the day.

These threads would be simple things like prayer beads in a pocket; a candle lit in a church when passing; the saying of the Angelus at midday; a glance at one of the devotional websites that offer daily prayer and reflection; a pocket size version of Old and New Testaments, Bible Reading Fellowship notes for a daily reading and reflection, or a book of prayers for the tube, train or bus, or kept next to the bed for reference before sleep. Like so many other aspects of life, it is through cumulative routine that things grow into depth, not through the grand gesture. As this rhythm of prayer and attention to God grows, so the time that we will want for it will naturally expand as well.

The cumulative pattern of taking note of the divine presence needs to be sustained and nurtured. It needs some sense of vision and purpose, a context in which it makes sense. The chores of washing, ironing, cooking, and ferrying children to and fro make sense in the context of home life and relationships. These chores are set in the perspective of wanting what is best for your children because you love them and in so doing you become more fully yourself. When sight of that perspective is lost, the chores become unbearable.

Somewhere in that perspective we also need to locate ourselves as still unique people with our own needs, in order to ensure that we are not submerged beneath an agglomeration of functions. There's nothing more dispiriting than when a child, or anyone else for that matter, asks, 'Why are you always in a mood?' The answer is often because there's nothing left that's sustaining and nurturing us. The rhythm of our life is shot to pieces; time is fully mortgaged, we feel loveless and alone, and there's nobody to tell.

Talk of commitment to God in this context always sounds just a little bit unattractive. When you're full to the brim with demands for your attention, another big one is the last thing you want. So in order to find our way into attention to the presence of God, I think we need a strand in the rhythm of our ordinary time that connects us consciously, but bearably, in ways I've suggested above. And we also need a perspective on handling this, some kind of a hold on the threads of eternity that we weave into our day, like the perspective that sustains the tasks of parenting, work, running the home, managing a social life, etc. We need an account of what these threads are in our daily noticing of God and how they bind us to God's eternity, like the way we are bound to a kite as it cavorts playfully in the wind, tugging persistently at our attention.

Let's return once more to the foundational documents of the Christian faith in the Old Testament in order to get a hold on the lines that bind time and eternity. We shall begin with a story that shapes the time frame, language and belief of both Christians and Jews. Next comes the angler's line, and the question of commitment comes into view. Here we consider first how God rescues us from death and then how we celebrate that liberation in our worship. We conclude the chapter with some reflections on the contrasting use of song and silence to describe the work of salvation and our participation in it.

Time for Eternity

In Genesis 22 God tests Abraham by asking him to sacrifice his son Isaac, the sign of their covenant. Abraham travels to the mountain in the land of Moriah as the designated place of sacrifice. He binds Isaac with rope, places him on the wood on the altar where the sacrifice will be offered and burned, and as he is about to kill the boy, an angel stops him. Although Abraham had been willing to offer his only son, God provides instead a ram for the offering.

For the early Church, this is a key story in the interpretation of what happens in the death of Jesus on the cross at Calvary. For the Jews in the early centuries of Christian history it is also an archetypal story that defines the pattern of all sacrifice. The offering is made as a statement of obedience and love towards God. It exemplifies the principle of representational offering – a lamb to represent a life. What is more challenging is the common reference to the sacrifice of Isaac as a bloodless offering, but a sacrifice nonetheless.

Here language is functioning in two ways. It is stating what is materially obvious: the blood of Isaac is not shed. At the same time it is asserting that Abraham's intention and action of binding Isaac is itself a sacrifice in which the shedding of blood is more than implied; it is, as it were, real. So we are saying, 'It is . . . and it is not.' The importance of this metaphorical device will emerge again when we consider the nature of the celebration of the Eucharist. But for the moment it is worth noting this device as characteristic of how Christian language and symbolism function as a means of speaking of and presenting reality we do not see, hear, touch or taste, but experience in all those ways.

So similar is some of the language in first- and second-century Jewish and Christian texts that it could prompt us to ask which tradition is influencing the other. But that discussion is a technical one for another occasion. What do the two traditions say about the binding of Isaac?

The binding of Isaac, called the *Aqedah*, features in one of the Jewish Targums, an interpretative translation into Aramaic of the Hebrew text of the Old Testament. The Targum describes it in the Poem of the Four Nights. It is an amazingly visionary account of all time suspended like dreams beyond the confines of this world, but real in the eternity of God. In these four nights four memorials are made. The first memorial is of creation, the second of Isaac's birth, the third of the Exodus, and the fourth of redemption by the Messiah. The whole of time, the history of creation, is held in these four episodes.

According to the poem, the memorials of what is in the eternity of God are celebrated at the time of Passover, which Christians observe as the time of the sacrificial death of Jesus on the cross. In the poem's description of the second night, the birth of Isaac, it states, 'And Isaac was thirty-seven years old when he was offered on the altar. The heavens were bowed and descended, and Isaac saw their perfections, and his eyes were dimmed because of their perfections.'

An adult Isaac suggests an even clearer connection with Jesus. Within the Jewish tradition a comment from elsewhere connects the blood of the Passover lamb with the blood of Issac's binding, reinforcing the link between Isaac and Jesus, whose blood is shed at Passover: God says, 'And when I see the blood [of the Passover lamb], I will pass over you (Exod.12:13) – I see the blood of Isaac's Aqedah.'[1]

In the Christian tradition the identification of the death of Jesus with the killing of the Passover lamb is most clearly indicated in John's gospel. The judgement by Pilate took place at about noon on the day of preparation for the Passover. Jesus, the Lamb of God, therefore dies at the same time as the sacrificial Passover lambs were being killed in the Temple. Further connections with the Jewish tradition mentioned above are found in the first letter of St Peter (1.20) and the Revelation of John (13.8). Both refer to the lamb slain since before the foundation of the world. Like the Poem of the Four Nights, this connects an event in time with the reality of eternity.

The early theologians of the Church place great emphasis on the binding of Isaac as an important statement about the redemption brought about by the binding of Jesus to the wood of the cross. About five hundred years after the birth of Jesus (that's still 'early' in Church terms) a French bishop, Caesarius of Arles, writes about the *Aqedah* in these terms:

> The ram that was stuck among the briars with its horns also seems to represent the Lord, for Christ as it were stuck among thorns with horns when he hung on the beam of the cross, fastened with nails. When Isaac carried the wood for the sacrifice of himself, in this too he prefigured Christ our Lord, who carried his own cross to the place of his passion.[2]

What is happening to our time frame here? As is often the case, the Christian theologian is suggesting a kind of concertina effect, whereby all time, past, present and future, is collided into the one earthly life span of Jesus. He is the recapitulation of human history, as another early theologian described it. So the event of the binding of Isaac in past time is being pulled into the point in time that witnesses the binding and sacrifice of Jesus. The binding of Isaac brings not only its own history (a story told again and again), but also the thread that connects it to eternity, as illustrated by the Poem of the Four Nights.

This binding, Jesus 'stuck' on the cross, describes in graphically contemporary language God's commitment to living in our flesh for the purposes of redemption. It will take God into the jaws of death itself. This is explored very early on in the Christian tradition in the letters of Ignatius, Bishop of Antioch. He lived at the end of the first century, and was among those who knew someone who had met one of the first disciples of Jesus.

In old age Ignatius writes to seven Churches, some of which, in Ephesus, Philippi and Rome, Paul had also addressed. Like Paul, Ignatius is also travelling to Rome, under arrest, to face execution. He was martyred in about AD 107 and his writings contain an insight and freshness that remain inspirational. In his letter to the Ephesians he writes:

Hidden from the prince of this world were the virginity of Mary and her child-bearing and likewise also the death of the Lord – three mysteries to be cried aloud – the which were wrought in the silence of God.[3]

The hiddenness of the identity of Jesus as God is what lies in the virginity of Mary, for this is the means by which God receives from Mary the one thing God does not have: flesh. The death of the Lord is not simply the death of another human being. Its significance is hidden from the sight of the prince of this world – a personification of evil. Our flesh is what veils and hides the glory of God when God the Son gives himself up to the experience of death and so accomplishes our liberation from death. (We shall consider the relationship between the silence of God and the Word of God that is spoken and heard in the person of Jesus Christ in the final section of this chapter.)

What we see in the stories about Isaac and Jesus is a statement about the threads that bind eternal reality to our lives. In one sense we don't need to do anything about that connection. The threads are there; they are God's work. Having a perspective on what happens at Calvary gives meaning and purpose to whatever rhythm of prayer we might be able to establish through our prayer beads, candles, etc. It is like what we do to keep a perspective on what's important about the home as a context of love and hope, and how that gives meaning and purpose to picking up the children from school, or beginning the working day at 5.00 am.

The connection between time and eternity is not ultimately of our making; it is there for our discovery and delight. Eternity is not dependent upon us, as though it were another chore. Part of our response to the apprehending of its existence is to ponder on how God shows us stuff, like the newness of eternal life. A conscious moment of becoming aware of the presence of God as part of daily life will foster our aptitude for pondering on what God reveals. It nurtures the unobtrusive growth of knowledge about the mysterious character of divine revelation, which has been described as 'unveiling, veilingly'.

The patience required for getting the hang of this process of revelation takes us back to the anglers along the River Wear. What do they have to teach us about the unfolding of divine love in God's commitment to the perfecting of creation?

An Invisible Thread

The point about sitting all day on a riverbank fishing with a rod and line is that on the end of the line is a hook hidden in the bait. The fish is attracted by the bait, swallows it and the hook, and so is caught. This very simple principle is essentially what Ignatius is describing when he speaks of the hiddenness of the mysteries that were to be cried aloud from the silence in which they were wrought by God. Two hundred and forty years later in Jerusalem a priest, Cyril, shortly to become the Bishop of Jerusalem, is using this illustration in his lessons to prepare candidates for baptism and confirmation.

The instruction is given in the church of the Holy Sepulchre. Although that wonderful building has been through many changes since St Cyril's time, the choir, where the Greek Orthodox community now celebrate the liturgy, is precisely where these classes were held. Cyril's point is a simple one:

The devil had used the flesh as an instrument against us . . . We were saved by the very weapons with which the devil fought against us. The Lord took from us a likeness to us, that he might save human nature . . . If the devil had recognized him, he would not have dared to approach him . . . His body therefore became a bait for death, so that the dragon, hoping to swallow him, might vomit up also those whom he had swallowed.[4]

The reference to a dragon is rather fluid in Christian imagery. But the overwhelming sense of the forces of chaos associated with the sea invariably leads to the presentation of the dragon as some kind of sea monster. We need only to think of Loch Ness to understand this. The sea beast named Leviathan in Psalm 104 is styled by the prophet Isaiah as the fleeing and twisting serpent, and thereafter its reputation is in tatters.

Doom paintings invariably show a sea beast opening its jaws as the gates to hell. In England traces of fifteenth-century doom paintings survive: St Clement, South Leigh, in Oxfordshire, and St Thomas, Salisbury, both have fine examples. Even into the late sixteenth century this beast haunts the religious imagination. El Greco's ambitious painting *The Adoration of the Name of Jesus* shows Leviathan in its traditional place, the bottom right hand of the painting as we look at it (on the left-hand side, the sinister side, of Christ in judgement).

But as Cyril indicates in his pre-baptism classes, the swallowing of God veiled in our flesh works like the hook on the end of the fisherman's line. Jesus, 'stuck' on the cross, as Caesarius puts it, caught like bait by the nails, in turn catches the death-dragon, Leviathan and beaches it. Stranded on the shore it is forced to open its mouth, because divinity within has brought about a terrible, fatal illness within death, and it 'vomits up' those it has swallowed. Ignatius described this moment as the abolition of the ancient kingdom of evil and the revealing of humankind in the newness of eternal life.

In the twelfth-century Winchester Psalter this episode of vomiting up the contents of the stomach of death is the way in which the artist represents the harrowing of hell. It reminds us that Jesus himself used the story of Jonah being swallowed into the belly of the whale to predict his own progress through death and into new life. The Psalter shows Jesus standing on the seashore with St Thomas and St Mary Magdalen, both witnesses of the resurrection, drawing out the souls who have been swallowed by death and liberating them back into life.

So it would appear that there's more to angling than meets the eye. As a metaphor for the work of our redemption, the line is an intriguing statement about commitment and how far we can stretch the patient love of God. God is both bait and line, and the extent to which God will be stretched out in order to make a catch is immeasurable, as is the strength required to reel in the catch for the purposes of salvation. This is the metaphor for a divine love that plays to our foibles of fickle interest and indifference; as any fly-fisherman knows, angling is also an exercise in very, very patient delicacy and skill.

An example of a different type of doom painting moves us on to how we might describe the human experience of being on the end of this divine line. On the stair of Burghley House there is one of the most extraordinary doom paintings in England. It's located on the ceiling of what is understandably known as the 'Hell Staircase' and was painted in the late seventeenth century by Antonio Verrio. The jaws of death yawn open to consume those who ascend the stairs, and descent is distinctly chilled by the sense of a narrow escape. In this instance the creature that devours us is a huge, demonic cat, darkly cruel and far from fluffy.

Evelyn Waugh uses the imaginary family of a House just such as this to articulate the drama of our life and death in his novel *Brideshead Revisited*. The novel is really a profound treatise on conversion and redemption, or 'the operation of divine grace', as the author himself puts it. Its third and final part is entitled 'A Twitch upon the Thread', a phrase that Waugh borrows from one of G. K. Chesterton's short stories about the priest and detective, Father Brown.

Waugh's story is narrated by Charles Ryder, a sceptic for most of the novel. Marchmain is the title of an aristocratic family. Brideshead is the name of the earldom that also belongs to them and the House that is their seat. The family's name is Flyte. Charles begins a connection with them in the 1920s when he meets the younger son, Sebastian, at Oxford. The novel was written by Waugh during the Second World War, and takes the form of Charles' recollection of adulthood prompted by a wartime posting to Brideshead.

The story is that Lord Marchmain left his wife and family to fight in Italy in the First World War and never returned. Instead, he established himself in Venice with an Italian mistress, Cara. Lord Marchmain's wife had been a Roman Catholic by birth (Waugh was a convert to Roman Catholicism). Lady Marchmain pre-deceased her husband, who had been required to convert in order to marry her, but she bequeathed her faith in very different ways to all four of her children. 'A Twitch upon the Thread' culminates in the return of Lord Marchmain to Brideshead to die.

The Flyte family is thoroughly aristocratic. It is also thoroughly dysfunctional in a way that is entirely modern, and so like any other we might know. Drink (no drugs to speak of), sex, pride, infidelity, introspection, rigid formalism, faith-seeking doubt, inconsiderate extravagance: these are all part of a glitteringly privileged story line that is also threaded with beauty, intelligence, grace, generosity and wit. The Marchmain life has reeled out the thread of divine love as far as a life of luxury can take it. The Marquis' impending death is the twitch upon it that will permit divine grace to draw this one exile back to his true native land – heaven.

As the family gathers around the deathbed, Julia, the elder daughter, calls for the Roman Catholic parish priest to prepare Lord Marchmain for death. It is not at all clear that her papa wants this, or is even still conscious. The priest arrives and begins the rite of anointing. Julia and Cara kneel and pray; Charles also kneels, out of courtesy, and silently articulates words that are quintessentially the prayer of our age: 'O God, if there is a God, forgive him his sins, if there is such a thing as sin.'

The priest continues his ministry and Charles hopes for a sign of response from Lord Marchmain; eventually it comes. With great effort he makes the sign of the cross, moving his hand from head to breast and across his shoulders. It was a silent but eloquent response to the priest's invitation to penitence. The twitch upon the thread is an indication that Lord Marchmain is incapable of resisting the joy of embracing the divine compassion that will enfold him as soon as he permits it to. Charles recognizes the significance of this immediately:

> Then I knew that the sign I had asked for was not a little thing, not a passing nod of recognition, and a phrase came back to me from my childhood of the veil of the temple being rent from top to bottom.[5]

He is helped to make the connection because of the setting of the deathbed scene. Of course the rite of anointing and commendation contributes significantly to that recognition, but the author's skill had in fact provided him with a more complex theological framework.

On his arrival back at Brideshead, Lord Marchmain had asked for the Queen's bed to be made up for him in a ground floor room. As the narrator of the story, Charles describes this bed as 'an exhibition piece, a vast velvet tent like the *baldachino* at St Peter's'. The reference is liturgical and theological, far more than it is an artistic one. It refers us to the practice in the ancient churches of the West of building a covering on four poles or columns around the altar. It seems that originally curtains hung within this structure and could be drawn at key moments of the liturgy. In a similar way the churches of the Orthodox East have doors in the screen in front of the altar that can be closed at key moments.

The point of the description of the bed as like a *baldachino* is that it invites us to identify what is happening on the bed at the moment of death with what happens on the altar in the Eucharist. There bread and wine, the signs of our life, are offered to God the Father in replication of the offering of Jesus. When Jesus says, 'this is my body', it is not only about the bread that he is speaking, or about his own body; he is also claiming the dead body of Lord Marchmain and every other child of God for his own or, we might say reclaiming them, from death.

Having been bait for the death-dragon, Jesus became the cause of the dragon's death. He then uses these words, 'this is my body', to call forth from its belly those whom it had swallowed. In one great continuum, the love of God is played out, literally, like the thread of a reel, expending itself further and further into the darkness of our death in order to call us out from the jaws of death and back to life.

'My life is yours' seems to sum up what Jesus is saying here, and in response we try to say the same: 'Your life is mine.' That was the commitment Lord Marchmain was struggling with. It is another way of stating what we say in repentance at baptism: 'I turn to Christ.' Nor is the intention of such a statement unintelligible to us in the process of ordinary human experience. From the intensity of human love we learn just how deep the certainty of mutual self-giving can go. Our experience of this depth is what we use to account for the depth of God's self-giving – only we know that God's is greater, deeper and eternal.

An expression of this depth comes from another product of the Second World War. It is a poem by Leo Marks, who was in charge of all codes and ciphers for agents working undercover in the Special Operations Executive. The poem is a centrepiece in the 1958 film *Carve her Name with Pride*, which tells the story of Violette Szabo, a young undercover agent. In the film Violette's husband, Etienne, writes the poem for her as her code. In real life Marks had written it for his girlfriend, who had just been killed in a plane crash, and the sentiment expressed is real and fresh:

> The life that I have
> Is all that I have
> And the life that I have
> Is yours.
> The love that I have
> Of the life that I have
> Is yours is yours is yours.
> A sleep I shall have
> A rest I shall have
> Yet death will be but a pause.
> For the peace of my years
> In the long green grass
> Will be yours and yours and yours.

Szabo was captured, tortured by the Nazis, and executed in 1945. She had given her life for the safety of those who were waging a war against the expansion of a regime of death and injustice. The 'yours' of her code and poem are her husband, their baby daughter, her parents, and those for whom she took a heroic stand for freedom. The life of Violette Szabo reveals a profound depth of love, personal, intimate, and wide-ranging in its care for humanity and its flourishing.

In such a love something can be read of the seriousness of how we might respond to the yet greater love of God. Martyrdom is not often asked of us; but the capacity to bear that vocation is part of the Christian inheritance. Does our formation in discipleship indicate this seriousness? Does our worship help us to live in such proximity to heaven that life on earth is a joyful rehearsal for that eternal reality?

Mysterious Simplicity

We noted in the previous chapter the significance of the rending of the veil of the Temple. That is a symbolic event that also points to seriousness. Waugh's reference to it at the death of Lord Marchmain ought to challenge us to reflect on how we do in fact connect the celebration of the Eucharist with our lives, with the fact of our death, and with the love of God. Even if martyrdom is not asked of us, it's fairly unlikely that we shall die in beds that look like something out of a baroque church. But the theatrical setting of our lives isn't really the way we connect them with the Eucharist.

We know and understand the seriousness of death. Its mystery cannot ever be explained away, and its presence ahead of each of us is a universal reality. The challenge is for our worship in church to be commensurate with the scope of this reality. The rending of the veil of the Temple is not simply an historical detail from the gospels; it ought also to describe what is torn open in our minds and hearts when the Eucharist is celebrated and heaven is laid before us. Here our death is made part of the hope of resurrection that is pledged to us, when we are able to say to God, 'The life that I have is all that I have, and the life that I have is yours.'

Over the past fifty years Anglicans and Roman Catholics have developed very similar ways of celebrating the Eucharist. In both cases we have seen some considerable achievements in releasing worship from a tired rigidity that was sapping its life. Simplicity, one of the aims of recent liturgical renewal, has a beauty that cannot be denied. It communicates more than itself and is not a reductive quality that eliminates profound meaning.

So, for example, people are fascinated by the abstract work of Mark Rothko because of its intense focus on colour as communication, even though its form is very simple in shape. Rothko's paintings communicate more than simply colour, more than themselves; they have the ability to determine the atmosphere of their environment. The content of his work is no less demanding and challenging than the very different style of Titian, for example, for whom colour is also very important, but whose form as a figurative artist is completely different in being explicitly complex. In a more obvious way the simplicity of Tate Modern has a nobility that is not undermined by the baroque splendour of St Paul's Cathedral on the opposite side of London's Millennium Bridge.

Contemporary patterns of celebrating the Eucharist run the risk of failing to achieve the simplicity that communicates more than itself. Instead, we may be guilty of a process of de-mystification that leaves us with little more than the reverberation of our own concerns. It would be unhelpful, I think, to go into detail of ceremonial and ornaments, or the lack of them. Perhaps a more telling indication is our attitude to the question of whether the Eucharist should be presented as essentially a meal. This is an example of the challenge that we face, as Anglicans and Roman Catholics, in getting the balance right between mystery and mystification, or between simplicity and superficiality.

The Eucharist is a meal, but it is also more than, and other than that. This matters greatly to Phil, a friend of mine, who is younger than I am, recently married, and completely in tune with the generation after mine. He works in the up-to-date, starkly unreligious world of media communications. He finds the language of a meal inadequate for what he wants to say about the Eucharist to his agnostic, atheist or (white, European) Buddhist chums.

In particular, Phil gives me a hard time about the phrase in one of the Eucharistic prayers that says Jesus 'had supper with his friends' the night before he died. This connects in Phil's mind – and his colleagues' minds – with a Friday or Saturday evening binge that may or may not involve a line of coke. It's a terribly middle-class, Islington or West Hampstead sort of phrase that does not easily convey the seriousness of how worship links life with death and resurrection, for example, or the majesty with which it should connect time and eternity.

I think Phil, and perhaps others of his generation, wants us to speak with more confidence about the 'mysteries wrought in the silence of God' that we in liturgy are called to 'cry aloud' through dramatic ritual. A meal is the symbolic medium for narrating those mysteries; it is not the mystery itself. A meal is part of that metaphorical dispensation that says of the altar as a meal table, in a phrase we have already used, 'it is, and it is not'. It is a stone or wooden table; it must also define and be the place where Isaac is bound, where the glory of God shines in mercy on the top of the ark of the covenant, and where Christ is crucified, glorified, and handed over to us in the Holy Spirit, as time and eternity intersect. And yet it is still a stone or wooden table. The bread of the Eucharist is bread, and yet it is not; it is specifically the body of Jesus, not in appearance but in reality.

Like the dream-world vision of the Poem of the Four Nights, our liturgy has to attempt to articulate with all the confidence faith can muster what is not visible in this world, even though we can only do so in broken sentences and humble gestures. Here all is seen through a veil, known by metaphor, represented by ritual drama. It is provisional until, as St Thomas Aquinas puts it:

> O Christ, whom now beneath a veil we see,
> May what we thirst for soon our portion be,
> To gaze on thee unveiled, and see thy face,
> The vision of thy glory and thy grace.[6]

These observations must not be read as criticism of the diligent priests and people who faithfully undertake the celebration of the

Eucharist throughout this land week by week. Their celebration, and every act of Christian worship, is a commitment to holding the ancient – and new – sacred places, for the sake of those who do not yet know the mysteries of life they represent, and for subsequent generations. But the challenge we face is formidable in many respects. We are trying to communicate with a culture that is seeking to evade the truth we wish to convey. The irony is that it is the truth we all long to know: where we come from, who we are, what we're for and who loves us.

Francis Thompson describes this situation in his poem 'The Hound of Heaven'. This is a different vision of God's self-binding and commitment, not in a fishing line, but like the pounding of a dog, relentlessly pursuing us across time and history as we flee from the divine truth and love:

> I fled Him, down the nights and down the days;
> I fled Him, down the arches of the years;
> I fled Him, down the labyrinthine ways
>   Of my own mind; and in the mist of tears
> I hid from Him, and under running laughter.
>   Up vistaed hopes I sped;
>   And shot, precipitated,
> Adown Titanic glooms of chasmèd fears,
> From those strong Feet that followed, followed after.
>   But with unhurrying chase,
>   And unperturbèd pace,
> Deliberate speed, majestic instancy,
>   They beat – and a Voice beat
>   More instant than the Feet –
> 'All things betray thee, who betrayest Me.'

God eventually tracks down the fleeing narrator of the poem and says, 'Rise, take My hand, and come!'[7]

One can almost hear the pounding of the hound's feet in the rhythm of each line. From that pounding comes a sense of our own breathing beginning to quicken as we race through long, densely constructed sentences. The urgency and terror of the chase of these lines indicate something of the experience of Francis Thompson's life as a vagrant drug addict on the streets of London. They also speak about the scope of all grief and loss.

I remember seeing part of a film on television about a young man and his girlfriend who had lived a life like Thompson's. They, too, were fragile in their love and addiction, and vulnerable to circumstance and crime. The most haunting moment was the closing sequence after Cass, the girlfriend, had finally been overwhelmed by the inevitability of death. Her boyfriend is seen lurching through an almost deserted Leicester Square in the very early morning, when bins were being emptied and deliveries made. He looked like, but wasn't, Pete Doherty, and the heart-rending memory is of his crying out his girlfriend's name, Cass, as though he could bring her back, or prevent her death.

This film was described as a love story wrapped in broken glass. The phrase captures the wounding nature of love and loss, and the pain of a searching grief that restlessly refuses to be comforted by the admission 'she is dead'. It also provides a point of reference for how we might describe the relationship between God and the human race that is characterized by similar episodes of loss, grief and searching.

Within its armoury of stories, the ancient world had one story that obviously suggested itself to the Church for adaptation to the Christian narrative about Jesus, who travels beyond the ends of the earth to rescue his bride from death. The story is that of Orpheus and Eurydice.

We have examined in closer detail what the line is like that binds us to God in the act of redemption and our celebration of it. As we pursue the story of Orpheus it is song and then silence that will emerge in our observation. Both have an important part to play in the binding of time, and our liberation from death.

Song and Silence

At the far eastern end of the northern Quire aisle in St Paul's there is a mosaic of Orpheus, the minstrel who charmed his way down to the underworld to rescue Eurydice, his wife, who had died from a snake bite. The goddess Persephone arranged for Eurydice to be released, but the condition was imposed that Orpheus must not look back to check that she was following him out of Hades, or she would return there. As they approached the gates of the underworld, Orpheus looked back in fear and anxiety, and Eurydice was taken from him for ever.

From the second century AD Jesus has been identified as a new Orpheus, leading his bride, the Church, out of the underworld. In this version of the story, the harrowing of hell is a musical event. In the catacombs in Rome there are five paintings of Jesus as Orpheus, the most graphic of them from the fourth century, in St Peter and St Marcellinus.

The second-century theologian, Clement of Alexandria, knows of this tradition, and observes wryly that while Orpheus was able to tame wild beasts with his music, Jesus tamed the wildest of them all: the human being. Unlike Orpheus, Jesus does rescue his bride, the Church, singing to her, writes Bersuire, a fourteenth-century monk in Paris, 'this verse from the Canticle of Canticles [the Song of Solomon] 2.10, "Rise up, my love, my fair one, and come away."'

To describe the expense of God in the work of creation and redemption as a piece of music is not in any sense to diminish its cost. It may be familiar to us from the hymn that concludes William Vanstone's book Love's Endeavour, *Love's Expense: The Response of Being to the Love of God*:

> Soaring music, tow'ring words,
> Art's perfection, scholar's truth,
> Joy supreme of human love,
> Memory's treasure, grace of youth;
>
> Open, Lord, are these Thy gifts,
> Gifts of love to mind and sense;
> Hidden is love's agony,
> Love's endeavour, love's expense.[8]

Part of the attraction of Vanstone's book lies in the title's ambiguous use of the word expense, meaning a cost but also a personal expenditure of energy and commitment.

In his book on icons and beauty, Paul Evdokimov makes a play on the word bios, the Greek word for life and for bow. He sees the stretching of the gut in the bow, an instrument of war, as transformed into life in the musical instrument of the lyre that produces harmony not discord. This transformation is identified with the work of Jesus, who, stretched on the cross, becomes an instrument (the pun is intentional) of harmony and new beauty.[9] This also becomes part of our vocation as Christians, who bear the likeness of Jesus Christ. In order to be instruments of peace in a discordant world, 'we must bear the pain of expansion,' writes Fr Benson, the founder of an Anglican order of monks, 'for we are stretched, indeed not ultimately on the rack of human torture, but on the glorious being of the Holy Ghost'.

We noted in Francis Thompson's poem the expenditure of God relentlessly seeking the poem's fleeing narrator. Like the disciplined expenditure required for sport, dance or drama, music requires its own stretching of our human capacities in order to produce something within us that has an origin beyond ourselves. Rowan Williams notes that this self-giving expenditure is also something we can identify with God: 'There is a sense in which God can be said to "exhaust" what he is in the mutual giving of the life of the trinity.'[10] This is an expenditure that is also described in Vikram Seth's novel *An Equal Music.*[11]

The narrator of the story, Michael, is a violinist. Playing in a concert that marks a turning-point in the story, he reflects, as though in a trance, on what is happening during the performance of a work by Haydn in the concert hall:

> so many disjunct parts: chairs, stands, music, bows, instruments, musicians – sitting, standing, shifting, sounding – all to produce these complex vibrations that jog the inner ear, and through them the grey mass that says: joy; love; sorrow; beauty . . . In front of us 540 half-seen beings intent on 540 different webs of sensation and

cerebration and emotion, and through us the spirit of someone scribbling away in 1772 with the sharpened feather of a bird.

Connections with the characterization of Jesus as Orpheus, and with Evdokimov's references to the bow and the lyre, are not difficult to find in this passage: bows and instruments, and sensations of joy, love, sorrow, beauty, all convey points of similarity. But the reference to 'the sharpened feather of a bird' is a more intriguing one.

It relates to the spirit of Haydn, a man long dead by the time of Michael's performance of his work. Something about resurrection hangs around the text at this point, as the novel indicates by Michael's subsequent recovery of an old love, albeit fleetingly. So the bird's feather takes flight, as it were, long after death, as the music lifts from the page in the performance Michael is describing. But how might this relate to us?

It is characteristic of Christian communities that we sing. St Augustine of Hippo is full of enthusiasm for this: 'Sing to the Lord a new song . . . Make sure that your life sings the same tune as your mouth,' he declares in one of his sermons. The songs that we sing are new songs, gospel songs. In this context 'new' is a way of describing what something eternal looks like when experienced in time.

Singing these songs, or saying them, but 'singing them with our lives', as Augustine suggests, is part of what the Church has always done in the daily Offices of Morning and Evening Prayer. This is a work that we undertake on behalf of the whole created order as part of our response to God in thanksgiving for the gift and miracle of creation.

Embracing the task of this daily recitation of songs, prayers and scripture readings is an expenditure in which Christians from many different walks of life do engage. And although it is a corporate prayer and work in which the whole Church participates each day, it is not dependent upon everyone being in the same place at the same time. It is done for the sake of the holiness of the Church and the conversion of the world in which the line of divine compassion is constantly being played out.

This is another thread that any Christian can hold as part of the rhythm for binding ourselves to the eternal life of God. Pope Paul VI described it as participation in 'the Canticle of Praise, unceasingly hymned in heaven and brought into this world of ours by our High Priest, Jesus Christ'. The point about this recitation of songs, like the performance that Vikram Seth describes, is that it brings alive through us the spirit of the composer, who in this case is God.

Applause is the reaction to a really good performance of music; it will even be the polite reaction to an indifferent or poor performance. The reaction of silence is altogether different. As disapproval it is incredibly stunning and incredibly rare. Silence has the capacity to draw all our activity and noise into a crucible from which some moment of profound experience might emerge. But the silence need not indicate disapproval; it can indicate the liberating expression of something much more beautiful.

In the summer of 2008 there were two performances of Mahler's Eighth Symphony in St Paul's Cathedral. It is a work that blends sacred and secular texts on a monumental scale, commensurate with the building in which it was being performed. Valery Gergiev brilliantly conducted the London Symphony Orchestra before a packed Cathedral on two successive nights.

The night I attended it was warm, and the audience had seemed unsettled as the performance began. The overwhelming grandeur of the piece welded us into a single body, so that when eventually the conductor's hand fell on the final chord there was an extraordinary moment of total silence. The quality of that silence is what I have in mind as the beautiful experience that emerges from the crucible.

This is a silence that begins to disclose to us how we might apprehend heaven. It may be moulded out of a company of disparate people who do not know each other. It may also be a silence that falls upon us when alone, emerging out of some unforeseen combination of factors that have brought about its happening, or it may be a whole congregation caught up in one single act of extended silent prayer.

The recognition of this universal ability to fall into silence should strengthen our patient claim that the ordinary experiences of human life are the location in which faith naturally stirs and grows. As we face the challenge of the expenditure needed for making this claim, I believe that this quality of silence is an important expression of how we make present in the present what is not flesh – what is God.

We are so used to noise being the normal environment in which we live, that silence becomes for us an alien terrain. In a similar way, not to believe in God has become the norm in this age: in our Western culture faith is a strange, alien practice. We are charged with finding ways to re-engage this culture with belief, or with a quality of silence in which the capacity to believe might stir.

Jeremy Begbie makes an interesting observation about the relationship between sound and silence in his book *Resounding Truth*. He comments that 'the final bars of Sibelius's Fifth Symphony are, in essence, silence punctuated by six chords'. But Begbie makes this point in the context of a wider discussion about our fear of silence as this features in contemporary song writing:

> In one of her songs, Alanis Morissette sings about:
> > The conflicts, the craziness and the sound of pretences
> > Falling all around . . . all around
> Then she challenges us:
> > Why are you so petrified of silence?
> > How can you handle this?
> And the music suddenly stops.[12]

If silence is the space in which we sense the stirrings of the capacity to believe, then this generation is likely to be afraid of it, because it is so foreign to us. But many of the things we fear tend to hold a fascination and attraction we find difficult to resist. Christian faith is no exception to this tendency. It is perhaps for this reason that remote places of pilgrimage and silence are increasingly popular among a wide range of people and for many different reasons. Lindisfarne, Iona, Walsingham, St Beuno's in Wales are all examples of where this interest flourishes.

'It is the wounds that God's stubborn, indifferent silence makes in language that alone make for memory and healing, as is found absolutely . . . in Christ's cry of dereliction and forsakenness.' That is a reflection from the theologian David Jasper, on his experience of the desert, and it is a good one for our purposes. It is precisely what Jeremy Begbie was saying about Sibelius' chords punctuating silence, only in reverse: our noise is punctuated by divine silence until the moment when from God there issues a final cry as on the cross at Calvary the bait is swallowed by death.

We noted earlier that Ignatius described silence as the context in which our salvation was wrought by the birth and death of Jesus. The wounding quality of this silence – wounding the human pride that expects God's response to us when we demand it – reminds us that the story of our salvation is also a 'love story wrapped in broken glass'. Here our jagged pride catches and tears the flesh of God on the cross, as God's silence punctures our pride's self-important, nervous chatter. Jasper suggests that once we have heard the silence of God, our language limps, rather like Jacob limps after wrestling with the angel of God at Peniel, only, says Jasper, 'it is no sin to limp'.[13]

This is a powerful metaphor that leads us, by way of conclusion, to a demonstration of how language can subsequently limp with grace and beauty as it accounts for the wounds that result from being battered by the silent love of God. This silence resides in the thread connecting time and eternity that will play out along the history of our lives, no matter how oblivious or hostile we may be to its existence. Such, we know, is the capacity of a parent's love, a metaphor for the love of God.

One of the great wordsmiths of the English language is John Donne. Through the turns and twists of his life, he feels the tug of the thread of love, both human and divine love, silently battering upon him, until at last, like Lord Marchmain, he can resist no longer. This is a fine example of language that limps with grace, as it articulates an experience of God for which no language is adequate:

> Batter my heart, three-personed God, for you
> As yet but knock, breathe, shine, and seek to mend;
> That I may rise and stand, o'erthrow me and bend
> Your force to break, blow, burn, and make me new.
> I, like a usurped town, to another due,

Labour to admit you, but O, to no end.
Reason, your viceroy in me, me should defend,
But is captived and proves weak or untrue.
Yet dearly I love you and would be loved fain,
But am betrothed unto your enemy.
Divorce me, untie, or break that knot again,
Take me to you, imprison me, for I
Except you enthral me, never shall be free,
Nor ever chaste, except you ravish me.

Three aspects of angling have provided the structure for our exploration of binding time: time itself, the line or thread, and song and silence. The first looked at the relationship between time and eternity in which we locate and energize our fleeting contacts with eternity, if fleeting they must be in busy lives determined by our other, proper loves. We then went on to consider how the story of the binding of Isaac develops our understanding of the relationship between time and eternity. The imagery that presented Jesus as the bait on the end of the line by which those lost in death would be recovered was used for our exploration of commitment, God's and ours, and presentation of this in liturgical celebration was recognized as a challenge in our engagement with secular society. In the third and final section we considered song as a reminder of the otherness of God in our culture, but also of the immediacy of heaven where, in silence, angels keep their ancient places.

Our fifth chapter, on celebration, will return to the subject of silence: the great silence of the Grande Chartreuse in the French Alps, the Mother House of the Carthusian Order. It begins, however, by considering how sound and sight relate to each other, before exploring what the visual equivalent of silence might be.

---

1 The comment is from the Mekhilta, an exegesis of the book of Exodus, and is quoted in Hayward, R. (1981), 'The Present State of Research into the Targumic Account of the Sacrifice of Isaac', *Journal of Jewish Studies*, XXXII, (2), 140–141. Professor Hayward argues for the existence of the *Aqedah* tradition prior to the time of Jesus, thus suggesting that it informed how Jesus understood his death on the cross. His argument makes a strong case against those

who claim that the *Aqedah* tradition is a much later one, dating from the second century. Acceptance of the later date is what might prompt us to ask whether the Christian tradition could have influenced the Judaic one. Whatever the answer, the debate itself is an indication that in the first two centuries AD the Judeo-Christian tradition attached huge importance to the binding of Isaac, the Passover lamb and the death of Jesus.

2   Caesarius of Arles, Sermon 84.3, in (1947–), *Fathers of the Church: A New Translation*. Washington, DC: Catholic University of America Press.

3   Epistle to the Ephesians 19, in Lightfoot, J. B. (1893), *The Apostolic Fathers*. London: Macmillan and Co., pp. 141–142.

4   St Cyril of Jerusalem, Catechetical Lectures, 12.15, in Bettenson, H. (1970), *The Later Christian Fathers*. Oxford University Press, p. 36.

5   Waugh, E. (1962), *Brideshead Revisited*. Harmondsworth: Penguin Books, p. 322.

6   From the hymn by St Thomas Aquinas, *Adoro te devote*, Thee we adore, O hidden Saviour, thee. Translated by Bishop J. R. Woodford.

7   Thompson, F. *Selected Poems of Francis Thompson*. London: Burns and Oates Ltd., p. 51.

8   Vanstone, W. (1977), *Love's Endeavour, Love's Expense: The Response of Being to the Love of God*. London: Darton, Longman and Todd, p. 119.

9   Evdokimov, P. (1990), *The Art of the Icon: A Theology of Beauty*. Redondo Beach, CA: Oakwood Publications, p. 13.

10   Williams, R. (2005), *Grace and Necessity: Reflections on Art and Love*. London: Continuum, p. 163. In the footnote Williams notes that 'the language of self-"devastation"' is used by the Russian theologian, Sergii Bulgakov in his work on the Incarnation. This observation deepens our understanding of the sense of Jesus being 'stuck' on the cross as the bait for our death.

11   Begbie, J. (2008), *Resounding Truth: Christian Wisdom in the World of Music*. London: SPCK, p. 285.

12   Seth, V. (2003), *An Equal Music*. London, Phoenix, p. 110.

13   Jasper, D. (2004), *The Sacred Desert: Religion, Literature, Art, and Culture*. Oxford: Blackwell, p. 52. The reference to limping is identified by Rowan Williams in Jacques Maritain's Mellon Lectures, *Creative Intuition in Art and Poetry*. The point will apply to art as we discuss it in the next chapter, and as Williams notes: Maritain 'speaks of finite beauty or finishedness in the work being always incomplete at some level, "limping", like the Biblical Jacob, from the encounter with what cannot be named; achieved art always has "*that kind* of imperfection through which infinity wounds the finite"'. Williams, *op. cit.*, p. 21.

14   Batchelor, M. (ed.) (1995), *The Lion Christian Poetry Collection*. Oxford: Lion Publishing, p. 26.

Chapter 5

The Art of Celebration

Restore to me, O Lord, the stole of immortality which I lost in the transgression of my first parents . . . May I be worthy of everlasting joy.

O Lord, you have said, 'My yoke is easy and my burden light': enable me to bear it so that I may walk in the strength of your grace.

Introduction

Bridges and their builders

Everybody loves London's Millennium Bridge. It really feels as though it's ours, and by that I mean ours as the walking public. There's none of the noise and pollution of cars, taxis, trains or buses; even bikes are banned, and quite right, I say. This is the fun-to-be-on, laughter bridge, where everyone wants to have their photo taken. Mates on an outing from work, grandparents, lovers, spouses, partners, tourists, children and students: they all want to get a snapshot of themselves on the wobbly bridge.

We love the Millennium Bridge because its history of spectacular failure makes it a very human sort of bridge. When crowds poured onto it in the first two days it was opened, it wobbled so badly it was promptly shut again. Two years and five million pounds later it re-opened, and has been a hit ever since.

The Millennium Bridge's wobble gives it a sense of quivering vitality that's just right for its purpose: to span the Thames in joining one of London's great institutions, Tate Modern, to one of its greatest buildings, St Paul's. There is real energy in this link because thousands use the bridge to visit both places on a day out. But there is also energy in the complementarity between what these two buildings enshrine: art and faith.

It may well be that art galleries and museums are the new cathedrals in our contemporary society, though they are also in fierce competition with shopping malls for this title. But these are not the places where people go when they need to mark or celebrate a national tragedy, triumph or moment of common rejoicing. Those are the moments when the nation still goes to church, and, wherever that church is, the people responsible for its mission and pastoral ministry must be attuned to the needs of the nation as it now is, with the diversity of faiths, belief and culture that constitutes British society.

St Paul's and Tate Modern are not in competition with each other for the nation's affection: we complement each other. Art galleries present the best of human creativity in their respective fields – contemporary or historical works of art. Their artists invite us to tell in words the story that art tells through paint, sculpture, film or event. We on our side of the Millennium Bridge have Christian stories to tell about human identity, purpose, limit and liberation, and we are constantly aware of how artists can illuminate this narrative for us. Illuminate, not illustrate. Illustration is a flat, static kind of one-to-one representation. Illumination suggests the possibility of seeing more than we saw previously, learning from one another in unexpected ways.

An example of this was the installation in St Paul's during a City of London Festival of two works by Yoko Ono. One was entitled *Morning Beams* and the other *River Bed*. *Morning Beams* suspended ropes from below a window on the eastern side of the North Transept and fixed them to huge railway sleepers on the floor, so that it appeared throughout the day that sun was streaming in through the window.

This was a work of art in the Japanese tradition. It nonetheless illuminated the Christian tradition, reminding us that each morning the Christian Church sings the praises of Jesus Christ as the sun rises in the sky because that sunrise is the metaphor of his resurrection and the gift of new life to us. The fact that these ropes were fixed to huge wooden beams only reinforced Christian symbolism, as the wood of the cross was identified in that fixing, and from those beams the angle of the ropes suggested an irrepressible sense of resurrection and ascent.

The installation was located in the chapel that is used in the summer for saying the Office of Morning Prayer. The illumination of our sacred space by Yoko Ono's work of art brought fresh awareness of the dynamics of our prayer and texts that could become dulled by routine. We could hear with renewed clarity the words of ancient hymns:

> O Christ the Light of heaven
> And of the world true Light,
> You come in all your radiance
> To cleave the web of night
>
> May steadfast faith sustain us,
> And hope made firm in you;
> The love that we have wasted,
> O God of love, renew.

River Bed offered a different kind of illumination about the nature of Christian faith celebrated in church. This work of art was an arrangement of large, smooth stones that invited some action to bring them to life. The viewing public actually performed that life-giving function by responding to the invitation to move a stone from its original location to one of two enclosures nearby. The first enclosure was where a stone could be placed in what would become a mound of sorrow, the second an altar of joy.

The sense of people building an altar of stones, for whatever purpose, is deep in the Judeo-Christian tradition. The Old Testament Patriarch, Jacob, the son of Isaac and brother of Esau, does this after his dream of the ladder between heaven and earth (Francis Thompson located its base in Charing Cross). The words of Jacob at his awakening are etched into the glass doors at the west end of St Paul's and they are the text associated with the dedication to God of every Christian church: 'This is none other than the house of God, and this is the gate of heaven.' (Genesis 28.17)

As I hope it has become apparent, many of the observations in this book about hands, mind, society, and life beyond the grave have been drawn from visual images in an attempt to illuminate these four themes. I hope that these images have engaged your interest and imagination. This hope is based on the fact that we are a very visual society. Phones now take pictures and play videos; adverts at bus stops and on buses have flashing lights and moving images; we don't write letters, we do YouTube instead.

All of this is great if in fact it stimulates our imaginative faculty, rather than making it lazy. Images are there as a bridge, to move us on from what we see to something beyond. It might move us to an insight into the artist's imagination or intention, to the political implications of the work of art's title, or it might simply be to outrage because deeply held convictions are being challenged. In Christian terms Max Ernst's 1926 painting of the Virgin Mary smacking the child Jesus would be an obvious example. Ultimately, the test of a work of art is the extent to which it is capable of moving us towards a different perception of reality.

But I sense a danger that the constant passing of images in front of us can dull the senses and slacken the imagination. It is absolutely right to enjoy for itself alone that which is seen, deriving delight and gratitude from the vision of this world and its potential for goodness and beauty.

This enjoyment is not being called into question, since heaven itself is described as the beatific vision of God. But within the bewildering variety of earthly images I suspect we miss what more there is, because we have lost the habit of imaginatively exploring those images with patient reflection and enquiry. The result is a wide, voracious hunger for images of newer, faster and brighter excitements, though few, if any of them, satisfy our longing.

How might this relate to our final chapter on art and celebration?

Celebration is art's counterpart and goal. The metaphor of the bridge is important here, and that's why the Millennium Bridge is more than a fun place; it is also a serious statement about transition. The relationship between art, imagination and faith that it represents is a fundamental expression of one way in which we are still capable of appreciating how God might be apprehended. Even if we have largely lost the habit of worship and the celebration of God's presence, the imagination continues to unfold itself within us, and can be the bridge to revitalized faith and trust.

A bridge of this kind is what links Heaven and Charing Cross. It invites the transition from a place of departure and arrivals, Charing Cross. Our destiny, however, is Heaven, a place that we have begun to know here on earth, and where we can experience a way of being alive that completes our present one. Departure and anticipated experience of it can begin now. Art is one means by which it is inspired; scripture is its book of codes, poems and meanings; celebration is its enactment.

We should also put down a marker at this point for the reality of what it is that inspires artists and closely links their work with that of God. In *Grace and Necessity* Rowan Williams notes that 'without art we should not fully see what *sanctity* is about'. Acceptance of this view relieves us of anxiety about the details of the artist's life, or even of his or her faith. It suggests that to speak of *Christian* art is really rather curious, as though other art had a different origin, not from God.

What stands out in Williams' perception of art is precisely the practice of something that has the quality of God-like revelation to it, not in the flat tones of predictable commentary, but in the fertility of bringing something real into existence. Williams continues:

> God's life exercises its own perfection in the imagining of a world into life, so that the exercise of the artist's imagination fills out what must be the heart of holy life for human creatures. The artist imagines a world that is both new and secretly inscribed in all that is already seen ('There is another world but it is the same as this one', in Rilke's famous phrase) . . . In this bestowing of life on self and world, the artist uncovers the generative love that is at the centre of holiness.[1]

Our point in this chapter is that artists and celebrants both play a role in uncovering 'the generative love that is at the centre of holiness'. We see this as the goal and purpose of attention to the work of our hands, minds, social presentation and future life. It is to this celebration that the preparatory prayers we have taken for our theme have been lead-ing us. We draw from the work of artists for the context in which our celebration happens.

The two concluding prayers that are our reference point for this chapter speak of immortality and a yoke made light. They are descrip-tions of the way in which the celebrant of the Eucharist speaks and acts in the name of Jesus Christ who is always *the* celebrant, the host of the party in which all celebrate with him. Later in this chapter we shall remind ourselves of how specific and distinctive roles exercised by one person can also be characteristic of us all.

In the Eucharist, the ministry of Jesus Christ the High Priest is exercised on earth by those who are called to it by God, chosen and authorized by the Church. But the whole people of God is also priestly and so every person will have a distinctive way of celebrating the mysteries of salvation in the Eucharist through the ordained per-son's particular vocation.

The point that concerns us here is the scope of this vocation as an expression of the Church's mission in the world. The Latin word for a bishop is *pontifex*. This means, literally, bridge-builder. It is exactly what we need for the Church's mission in our own day. A bishop is the chief celebrant of the unit of Christian mission, the diocese. The bishop, with those who share the priestly office, models the ministry of Jesus Christ who gives his life for and with others. The bishop is likewise to be the person whose life is expended for others, in order to be a living bridge, vital, loving, human, strong, compassionate, wob-bling with joy and laughter, and generous in the invitation to set out on the journey to an eternal celebration. This is the ministry through which the whole Church invites those who have not yet been graced with faith to use us, the priestly people of God, as a bridge into a truer perception of our shared world.

Celebration is therefore what we are for. It is our destiny and the culmination of the work of our hands, the exploration of our minds, the dressing of ourselves in dignity, and the recognition of the life beyond the grave. 'To be worthy of everlasting joy' is the preparatory prayer of our lives; that kind of celebration is where our vested interests ultimately lie. This is not a celebration of our own achievements, but a celebration of the gift of life perfected into fullness. Delight in that life would be another phrase to describe it; bliss is also a word often used instead of celebration, as is consummation.

How can we begin to get the hang of how our present loves and best selves are only the start of something more intense, more enduring and delightful? This eternal celebration is (in the strict sense, not James Bond's usage) divine. Like God, this celebration needs no other justification. It is a symptom of being with God, characteristic of the divine expenditure that we noted in the previous chapter.

Words alone are insufficient for the expression of this celebration, so art offers a parallel narrative to help words out. But just as words cumulatively cannot exhaust what we might wish to say about eternal and perfect celebration, so also art reaches its own boundaries. It does so in ways that are akin to the reduction of words to silence. The richness of visual images can find its fulfilment in brilliant, blinding light and dazzling darkness. This is not a blindness of despair, but something that results from an overpowering experience that leaves us elated, stunned and silenced.

Some insights into this dazzling experience emerge in sections 1 and 3 of this chapter, as we consider the work of two artists that we would describe as modern, though they belong to different centuries, Wassily Kandinsky in the last century and Antony Gormley in this one. Neither sets out to present explicitly Christian works of art, but, like Yoko Ono's installations, both provide us with a rich and profound understanding of the celebration of heaven. Section 2 will consider the application of the artistic vision to life as some people actually live it. In each case we shall see how art/life invites transition, sets up a bridge that invites us to move on into a different realm. Thus art rehearses in temporal, and not necessarily explicitly Christian, ways the adventure of baptism and the life of Christian pilgrimage.

Following these explorations, we shall conclude this book with a reflection on who will be in heaven, and what it might be like there.

Art in Transition

1 The sound of colour

In 2006 Tate Modern mounted an exhibition of work by the Russian artist Wassily Kandinsky; St Paul's responded to the visual feast on one side of the Thames with a musical banquet on the other. Music had had a profound effect on Kandinsky, a performance of Wagner's *Lohengrin* being one of the experiences that convinced him in 1896 to become an artist. In 1911 Kandinsky was again arrested by music, this time that of Arnold Schoenberg. The Three Piano Pieces, op. 11, the String Quartet no. 2, op. 10, and Six Little Piano Pieces, op. 19 all contributed to Kandinsky's Path to Abstraction – the title of the Tate Modern exhibition.

The exhibition's plotting of this stage of Kandinsky's art was like being got ready to fall into a swimming pool. At one moment you are walking along and everything around you is more or less normal: objects have a clear form and shape; you can see what they are. Gradually, the form begins to become more fluid; shapes dissolve their boundaries, like the way light is broken when it hits the moving water of a pool. Eventually you tumble into the pool. Form, shape and order blur. Senses, in the way they functioned on the edge of the pool, are suspended. But they re-form, as light, buoyancy, movement, momentum, sound and feeling take on a different character.

Here the artist invites transition of a different sort. But the point of finding oneself in a different dimension, where our body and senses yield strange experiences to us, is not so inappropriate as a description of the experience of God in prayer and in the threads we considered in the previous chapter that relate to earth and heaven. Immersion in water is the primary image of Christian initiation in baptism. It is a symbol of leaving all behind in order to find a new life. The point about it is that on emerging from the pool of baptism one sees things differently. The model for this is Jesus: 'And just as he was coming up out of the water, he saw the heavens torn apart and the Spirit descending like a dove.' (Mark 1.10)

Kandinsky's painting *Impression III (Concert)* is a wonderfully vivid example of this tumbling into the abstract, in which objects begin to lose their definition as form and colour, and they coalesce in a new order. There are large amounts of colour (yellow, orange, black and some stretches of purple) that seem to be unaccounted for as any kind of object, while blurred figures, some with clearly defined but not immediately recognizable shapes, occupy a middle ground. For Kandinsky this was not simply a movement into abstraction; he was also moving into an experience of art in which he could hear the sound of colour. It is a sensation that Kandinsky describes in his book Concerning the Spiritual in Art, originally published in German in 1912.

Here are some of the ways Kandisky describes the sound of colour:

Yellow, if steadily gazed at in any geometrical form, has a disturbing influence, and reveals in the colour an insistent, aggressive character. The intensification of the yellow increases the painful shrillness of its note.

Kandinsky also provides a footnote to remind us that 'the sour-tasting lemon and shrill-singing canary are both yellow'.

Blue is the typical heavenly colour. The ultimate feeling it creates is one of rest . . . In music a light blue is like a flute, a darker blue a 'cello; a still darker a thunderous double bass; and the darkest blue of all – an organ.

Light warm red has a certain similarity to medium yellow, alike in texture and appeal, and gives a feeling of strength, vigour, determination, triumph. In music it is a sound of trumpets, strong, harsh, and ringing.

A cold, light red contains a very distinct bodily or material element, but it is always pure, like the fresh beauty of the face of a young girl. The singing notes of a violin express this exactly in music.

Violet is red withdrawn from humanity by blue . . . It is consequently rather sad and ailing . . . In music it is an English horn, or the deep notes of wood instruments (e.g. a bassoon).

All of these observations provide us with invaluable information for reading Kandinsky's abstract paintings. They are, if you like, a guide to the experience of being in the swimming pool and how our sensory perceptions might function differently. But two colours he describes do not have a sound attached to them in the way that the other colours have. We have already encountered their sound in the previous chapter.

Kandinsky describes the colour black as 'the silence of death'. This is like our suggestion that the response of silence could express dislike of, or even anger at, a piece of music, perhaps because badly performed. More importantly for our purposes, however, is Kandinsky's description of the colour white:

> White . . . is a symbol of a world from which all colour as a definite attribute has disappeared. This world is too far above us for its harmony to touch our souls. A great silence, like an impenetrable wall, shrouds its life from our understanding. White, therefore, has this harmony of silence, which works upon us negatively, like many pauses in music that break temporarily the melody. It is not a dead silence, but one pregnant with possibilities.[2]

Kandinsky's view of whiteness suggests something more dynamic than Robert Frost was proposing in Chapter 2, in his description of snow as a 'blanker whiteness . . . with no expression'. But the two descriptions need not be in conflict with each other. Also in that chapter we noted how the young man Motovilov saw snowflakes falling during his encounter with the transfigured St Seraphim as ignited by blinding light. We could expect Kandinsky to understand that in his own Russian tradition blank whiteness becomes the sign of transfiguration. This suggests to us that for Kandinsky, Robert Frost and St Seraphim the silence of the colour white is not the silence of death implied by the colour black; it is the colour that is 'pregnant with possibilities'.

Robert Frost had spoken of fear as characteristic of his reaction to the desert places suggested by a snow-covered terrain. In a similar way, our fear of silence is fuelled by not knowing what it might hold, though we are aware that it could be 'pregnant with possibilities'. In the previous chapter Jeremy Begbie commented on this in the lyrics of Alanis Morissette, and the description David Jasper used of a wounded language that limps like Jacob after his encounter with God, added to the impression of silence as a source of fear because it challenges our futile noisiness.

What we fear is the task of scaling a seemingly insurmountable wall to discover what the possibilities are that this pregnant silence holds. This fear is perhaps the reason why the second stage of preparation for worship asks for the protection of a helmet of salvation. Only with the confidence of such protection might we embark on investigation of the impenetrable wall of God's silence.

This may sound all very theoretical and far-fetched. You might even wish to suggest that, living in central London, I should get out more. The enjoyment of cultural and social privileges lies in the knowledge of their character as gifted by God. These gifts should also point us towards our ultimate destiny, the celebration of heaven, for which we have a borrowed nostalgia in the expectation of life beyond the grave. Our next example of art in transition offers a very different way of making the transition to the celebration of heaven; it makes the living of life an art form of self-forgetfulness and self-fulfilment.

2 White: the colour of silence

The introduction to this chapter suggested that people called to different vocations in the Christian life represent to us a truth about the whole Church, although only some of this truth may be lived out distinctively, in its fullness. For instance, priesthood, missionary work, marriage, and life in a religious order are all expressions of something to which not everyone can be called. But each distinctive expression should in some way characterize all of us.

The whole Church is priestly, called to offer praise and thanksgiving to God as servants and agents of reconciliation, just as this is exemplified in some who exercise ministerial priesthood through ordination. Similarly, some are called to leave home in order to be missionaries for the gospel that all Christians are duty bound to preach in the manner of how we live our lives.

All Christians, irrespective of their marital state or sexual orientation, are called to an understanding that the whole of life is sacred within the marriage bond of earth and heaven as it is constituted by the incarnation of Jesus Christ. Within this bond we are all asked to fashion homes that model the life of Nazareth, the hospitality of the kingdom, and the extension of ourselves in relationships, not only with those we love, but with all humanity in whom we seek to find the face of Jesus. Those who are married have the responsibility for ensuring that their distinctive fostering of these values provides an environment that enables children to grow up with the experience of them as the norms of Christian living.

The living of a distinctive life in a religious order, governed by monastic vows of stability, conversion of life, and obedience, or by what are known as the evangelical counsels – chastity, poverty and obedience – should also characterize the life of the Church as a whole. The use of sex, money and power in ways that are fruitful, authentic, safe, just, and transparently Christ-like is not a task we entrust to monks and nuns so that we don't have to do it.

These vows and counsels are, of course, the basis of the vocation to a very distinctive form of engagement with the realities of the world. Those who bind themselves to it exercise a freedom to model its potential for the sake of the whole people of God. But Christians called to different vocations that properly have other responsibilities and demands should also exemplify the qualities of monastic life in some fashion that is appropriate to lives lived in the world and lived for its salvation.

That said, I wish to concentrate on a significant element in the religious life, one which is easily overlooked – and that is the mystery of silence. Silence has featured prominently in earlier chapters. In Chapter 2 we noted Karl Rahner's observation that silence on earth is the true medium for conveying on earth the sound of heaven. This pattern of reversal was further accentuated in the previous chapter by Jeremy Begbie's comment about punctuated silence in Sibelius' Fifth Symphony and David Jasper's allusion to Michel de Certeau that we mentioned above. How does the genius (in the sense of a prevailing character or spirit) of silence in the life of some religious orders connect with those of us whose discipleship is in the noisy world?

In December 2006 a film by Philip Gröning, entitled *Into Great Silence*, was released in British cinemas. It was an almost entirely silent documentary about an almost entirely silent religious community, the Carthusians, and their mother house, the Grande Chartreuse, in the French Alps.

Gröning had first asked if he could film the community in 1986. The matter was considered but the community felt it was 'too early' for such an invasion into their lives. The last photographic record of the Grande Chartreuse had been in 1960. They asked for ten or fifteen years to consider the request. Eventually, after a relationship of trust had grown between director and community, the cameras were allowed in.

This detail about the permission of the community is crucial to the film itself, because it tells us so much about the time frame with which they work. There is something refreshing about so serious a resistance to the prurient eye of the camera, the celebrity status it is capable of bestowing, and the possible cheapening of dignity when people's lives are turned into entertainment. When so much of our life expects answers on demand, the request for a fifteen-year consideration is breathtakingly daring.

Although my sympathies would perhaps obviously and easily rest with the Carthusians on this matter, it is evident that I was not alone in my interest in the film. One of the extraordinary things about the release of *Into Great Silence* was the attention it attracted, especially from young people, the vast majority of whom appeared to have no religious affiliation or interest. (This is an entirely subjective judgement, and I'm ashamed to say made on the basis of a sort of 'anorak' assessment of what is characteristic and peculiar to church-going habits in Britain.) For the duration of nearly three hours, the film drew utter stillness and silence from an absorbed audience packed into a large auditorium.

These may be interesting points to note, but what of the film itself? Being set in the French Alps, snow featured prominently and often. The Carthusians wear a white habit of heavy-duty cloth, live in large, white houses, and worship is an austerely unadorned church. The atmosphere of their life is in so many respects described by Kandinsky's account of the colour white. Here there is indeed a colour scheme that suggests silence pregnant with possibilities.

The monks are like architects committed to the edifice of this silence, learning to understand its structure and how to move around and within it. They are dedicated to tackling how to scale the immense wall of the ineffable presence of God, simply because, as human beings, they can. That is God's gift to us. In this respect the monks are very like mountaineers who hang precariously from icy rock faces in search of something almost unnameable – because they have the capacity, imagination, strength and desire to do so.

Although the film is long by normal standards, there is little sense of action or story line. What emerges most powerfully is the aptitude that the camera has learned for pondering on what happens, even in small detail. Holy water that the monks use to make the sign of the cross in memory of their baptism as they go into the monastic church is seen to come to rest in the stoup after being disturbed.

The molecular structure of seeing water on stone becomes another image that invites patient reflection into its meaning. In this case it will relate the mystery of creation to the spiritual potential of baptism, and what enables these monks to live lives of heroic, prayerful silence, and the material possibility of how water sustains the crops they grow for their food. These issues – prayer and food – confront us all.

The silence is broken by the spoken word only at the end of the film. There is an interview with an ancient monk who is blind and close to death. Remembering what we said earlier about reversal of sound and silence, this interview is brilliantly well thought through. Those who are still actively living their monastic life and as yet remote from death, the gateway to reality, remain silent and removed from us. Only one, who is imminently engaged to life beyond the grave, comes close to us and speaks. We, the seeing, who watch the film are, in our culture, generally afraid of death. This man, who is blind, sees its meaning and is not afraid at all. 'Why be afraid of death?' he asks. 'The past, the present, these are human things. With God there is only present.'

We recognize that God had already become that blind monk's

present. Here is an example of transition to heaven, crossing the bridge that the spiritual imagination has formed as a work of art in the structure of monastic life. This is life lived as a kind of art installation of eternity. Through the discipline of silence, heaven is heard; in the singing of the Canticle of praise, by day and night (literally), time is sanctified, so that it becomes virtually possible to live in the celebration of God's present.

Philip Gröning shared the life of the Carthusian community for several months while the film was being made. He noted that it was a life unchanged in ten centuries. There is no anxiety about career structure, or the future, just the freedom for appreciation of the earth, its seasons, its fruitfulness, its beauty and other people.

The film also shows us one of the days, in the winter, when the monks go out to ski. They play unaffectedly like children, before returning to silence and waiting on God. One gets the impression that these silent, sentient, disciplined men have more idea and experience of celebration than we do, even with all the delights of London culture on our doorstep.

We might also want to reflect on what model of masculinity these monks are offering Western society's male population. The monastic life suggests a sociability that is centred on mutuality, not competition, and though these Carthusians are clearly strong-minded men, their strength is not combative in their dealings with each other. They seem to have little anxiety about dealing with their bodies, demonstrated by the arrangements for cutting each other's hair and caring for their infirm brothers. Nor do they appear naïve about relationships, modelling a form of male bonding that is unselfconsciously affectionate and held in balance with their commitment to a community of brothers who nonetheless live an essentially solitary life.

Gröning explains that within this expression of monastic life there's a very simple concept; he describes it as the exceptional vocation to Carthusian life, and it is centred on what we have termed celebration. 'The concept is God, pure happiness,' says Gröning; 'the closer you move to God, the happier you are.' Were it not for the steely discipline of silence, the life of prayer, and the environment-friendly simplicity that prompted this statement, it would sound trite. As it is, few of us sustain a life that more amply demonstrates its truth.

When we become anxious about our future, the scriptures are simple and lovingly stern: 'To-day if ye will hear his voice, harden not your hearts' is the way the Psalmist puts it. 'Harden not your hearts' is one way of talking about what today we call stress induced by pride and greed. 'Chill out, and don't be anxious: here, today, is merciful judgement and salvation' is more or less the way it translates. What is our response?

Do those you love, know you love them? Are your dealings at work and at home ready for inspection? When did you last smile, just because you are alive? When did you last watch the sun go down or a huge harvest moon rise over the Millennium Bridge or your equivalent? We are party animals who know how to binge, but we have forgotten the art of sustained celebration.

The blind monk saw that all time belongs to God and is entrusted to us for our benefit. By its right use we can liberate time from oppressing us and sanctify it by punctuating its transition with praise and thanksgiving. In a film that was often lit only by flickering candles, the words that are spoken at the Easter Vigil when the great paschal candle is lit come easily to mind: 'Christ yesterday and today, the beginning and the end, Alpha and Omega, all time belongs to him, and all ages; to him be glory and power, through every age and for ever.'

The impact of this on us as people in an age that is fidgety and neurotic about itself, uncertain of its past and fearful of its future, should be the calming of our anxiety and lessening of our haste. The timetable of the Carthusian monastery for giving permission to film its life ought to be something of a challenge to us. This is well articulated by Anthony Burton, the Bishop of Saskatchewan: 'When the Church takes account only of the present, she does nothing but change; if she looks only to the future, she does nothing but dream; only when she is conscious of being the living tradition of Christ is she truly renewed.'[3]

The colour white and a silence that is pregnant with heavenly possibilities are the artistic prompts to our generation. They encourage us to recover the art of transition to a life beyond the confines of this one and into the eternal celebration of our future. The takings of cinemas where *Into Great Silence* was shown suggest that we are 'up for it'. So do the numbers queuing to see the art shows in our galleries. What is it they want to see? An answer to that question will complete this chapter on blending colour, sound and movement, leading us to the conclusion of the whole book with the question of who else is in the celebration of heaven.

3 *Blind Light*

One of the things that people really have wanted to see recently was Antony Gormley's exhibition Blind Light, which we mentioned in the introduction to this chapter. The exhibition was centred at the Hayward Gallery in London, but one work that was part of it, *Event Horizon*, located 27 figures on buildings all around the South Bank. These were intended to prompt us to see ourselves in a new way in relation to the built environment, and to ask questions about isolation and lostness in the city.

Having a part of the exhibition inside the Gallery located outside the building was also a conceit that was continued in the show itself. *Blind Light* was a square room that was filled with cloud. What should have been outside, the weather, was inside. Here immediately we see art functioning as transition, taking us into a space only to discover that in it is the outside. But when linked with the narrative of Christian tradition and worship, this inside-out installation makes perfect sense. It illuminates our experience of God. How does this happen?

In an interview with Antony Gormley, Ralph Rugoff, the Director of the Hayward Gallery, describes *Blind Light* as being like a piece of modern architecture, a Bauhaus structure, with this 'cloud of unknowing' within it. The reference was unacknowledged by Rugoff, but it alludes to the title of a late fourteenth-century treatise on the Christian life. The opening of that treatise states in terms that are familiar to us that the fourth stage of Christian life 'may be begun here, but it goes on for ever in the bliss of Heaven'.[4] We are talking in similar terms about the nature of transition, from here to heaven.

The experience of going into Blind Light was extraordinary. The cloud that filled the chamber was brilliantly light. Visibility was almost nil and one was dazzled by the light. The effect was disorientating, as Gormley intended, and explained to Rugoff: 'You enter this interior space that is the equivalent of being on the top of a mountain or at the bottom of the sea.'[5] These references connect in the Christian tradition with the context in which Moses speaks to God on Mount Sinai, and remind us of the fearsome Leviathan, of whom we spoke in the last chapter.

The notion of encountering God in a cloud translates itself into the heart of the worship of the people of Israel in the Temple that Solomon builds. As with the worship in the temporary structure of the Tent of Meeting that had been used throughout the pilgrimage of forty years in the wilderness, incense is how a cloud is replicated and the presence of God is celebrated. When the Temple is dedicated, the Holy of holies, a square room – like Gormley's Bauhaus structure – is so filled with cloud that we could imagine the disorientation was like being in the Hayward Gallery: 'the house of the Lord was filled with a cloud, so that the priests could not stand to minister because of the cloud; for the glory of the Lord filled the House of God.' (2 Chronicles 5.13–14)

I visited the exhibition with a friend of mine who is a lawyer. He didn't like the look of *Blind Light* at all. It was just what lawyers disapprove of most: loss of detail, control and orientation. Having already gone in myself, I insisted he go in as well and I waited outside with his briefcase containing confidential documents. While waiting, I was intrigued to hear the comments from other people inside. Most people were fairly young, it seemed – by chance, I think. Apart from a lot of stuff about 'I'm lost' and 'Where are you?' and 'How do you get out?' there were two really interesting comments: 'It's like heaven' and 'I want to dance'.

The comparison with heaven seemed to be an unconsciously Christian reference, though that was a subjective assessment on my part. But the allusion was spot on as a statement about an earthly experience of something that transports us beyond ourselves. The connection with dance strongly reinforces this.

In *God and Grace of Body* David Brown explores at length the place of dance in Jewish and Christian traditions.[6] It is refreshing to read a serious exploration of an important artistic genre that has not been well served by some popular forms of liturgical dance. But the recent inclusion in an exhibition at the Royal Academy, London, of Henri Matisse's painting *Dance*, from the State Hermitage, St Petersburg, might have done something to rekindle our interest in this genre.

Brown points out that the dancer's leap is a metaphor for resurrection. It is a temporary departure from the earthbound nature of life as we know it, into a different zone or place of experience. This transition is what Matisse captures brilliantly. One art critic called it 'the most beautiful painting of the modern world'. But there is one detail in it that connects the painting with the comment I heard in Gormley's *Blind Light*. In Matisse's paintings of the five dancers who circle each other, there is always a break somewhere between them; the hands are not all connected. We are invited to join the dance.

The observation about dance from the person in *Blind Light* is, perhaps, a coincidental one. But it is not invalid. It accurately identifies the Biblical association of dance with the worship before the ark of God and the ark's home in the Temple. King David and all the house of Israel dance before the Lord as the ark enters Jerusalem (2 Samuel 6.5). The Psalms, the hymns of the Temple, also make the connection: 'O sing unto the Lord a new song . . . Let the children of Sion be joyful in their King. Let them praise his Name in the dance.' (Psalm 149.1–3)

More important than any theological intention in the comments about heaven and dancing that I heard from inside *Blind Light* was the fact that this installation inspired such comments. Art was functioning here as a point of transition. In that 'inside-out' box of light, perception of a different way of being was invited. Faith grows precisely out of the recognition that the world, life, knowledge and other people always constitute more than we know; difference awaits us. Words at the end of *The Cloud of Unknowing* would encourage us across the bridge of discovery that art inspires, as we think about what God might make of us: 'It is not what you are or have been that God looks at with his merciful eyes, but what you would be.'[7] The question of what we would be is one to which the preparatory vesting prayers for Eucharistic celebration have been leading us.

We began this chapter on art in transition with Kandinsky and the transition into abstraction in which colour conveyed sound. *Into Great Silence* took us to an example of the application of the colour white to real life in which we discovered transition into the eternal present of God. Antony Gormley's *Blind Light* has taken us back into the Christian tradition of dazzling darkness that is the prelude to our experience of heaven.

All three demonstrate ways in which art prompts our imagination, where the capacity for faith resides. All three inspire some form of transition, in which the *pontifex*, the bishop, or bridge-builder, enables the Church to be fully itself in the celebration of worship and liturgy that characterize the goal to which the bridge leads us: heaven itself. We now come to draw some conclusions, both to this chapter and to the book as a whole, by asking who is in heaven and how are we connected with that society.

1   Williams, R. (2005), *Grace and Necessity: Reflections on Art and Love*. London: Continuum, p. 167.

2   Kandinsky, W. (trans. Sadler, M.) (2006), *Concerning the Spiritual in Art*. London: Tate Publishing, pp. 74–81.

3   Burton, A. (2008), 'The End of the Liturgical Movement and the Recovery of Biblical Worship: An Anglican Perspective', *Faith and Worship*, 62, 37.

4   Walters, C. (ed.) (1961), *The Cloud of Unknowing*. Harmondsworth: Penguin, p. 51.

5   Vidler, A., Stewart, S. and Mitchell, W. J. T. (eds) (2007), *Antony Gormley: Blind Light*. London: Hayward Publishing, p. 55.

6   Brown, D. (2007), *God and Grace of Body: Sacrament in Ordinary*. Oxford University Press, pp. 61–119.

7   Walters, C., *op. cit.*, p. 144.

Conclusion

On earth as it is in heaven.

One of the major contributions that Antony Gormley has made to society through his art is the challenge to look again at what the scope of the human person is. We are fearfully and wonderfully made; that is the Christian conviction and it has been the tenor of the prayers that form the spine of these reflections. If people who had no experience of Church discovered in church an invitation to seriousness about what they would wish to be, with some expectation of its perfect accomplishment, I think we could make progress towards a restoration of the practice of belief and trust in God.

The vesting prayers that prepare us for celebration turn our attention to the unity of the human person and what we would be. We are not simply an organism that can perform a series of functions. The lecture by Professor Jeeves that we considered in Chapter 2 gave us good reason to withstand such a limited view of our life.

The prayers, by contrast, suggest aspects of our life that constantly open up more than might appear at a superficial level. In the Eucharist Jesus bequeathed to us we gather as his disciples to celebrate what makes us most fully ourselves: Christ in our midst. These key aspects of ourselves – hands, mind, body, life – offer definition to our participation in the Eucharist and the scope of its fulfilment in heaven. In a curious way, I think that the experience of working with people who have mental illness or are suffering from dementia illustrates this well. We are, understandably, nervous about relating to these conditions that so powerfully obscure human identity.

Perhaps it is worth noting that in the Paralympics we quite properly celebrate the achievements of people whose life is different in physical ways. But what celebration is there that testifies to the existence of the human person that is lost from our view through mental illness or dementia? It is here that the integrity of the human person as characterized fundamentally by mystery should make us pause.

The burden of losing someone we have known, respected and loved to an unknown place within the kingdom of their own minds is painful and it is exhausting in the demands they can make. But this also seems to me to indicate something of how we might describe the transition from earth to heaven. The recognizable contours of our earthly, physical existence are in place. The hands that have caressed us are the same, as are the voice, the eyes, and, tantalizingly, at times, the mind. But there is another place to which that person has gone, a place to which we cannot go within the terms of our present dispensation. We can only love them for having been with us, in the belief that something between us has not changed, cannot be lost, and will, finally, be restored, when we are all, once again, dressed and in our right minds.

This nostalgia for the wholeness of ourselves, made particularly poignant when we see it fragmented in others, prompts consideration of one final work of art that describes the reality of celebration in heaven and the way we image it on earth.

El Greco painted *The Burial of the Count of Orgaz* between 1586 and 1588 in the Chapel of Our Lady of Concepción, where the Count is buried, in the parish of Santo Tomé, in Toledo. In some respects it is El Greco's greatest statement of the relationship between earth and heaven, and his finest work.

The story of the burial of the devout and charitable Count was never accepted as a miracle, though. It was claimed that when his body was being lowered into the earth, St Augustine of Hippo and St Stephen appeared from heaven and took charge of the burial of the Count's earthly remains, while he himself was carried by angels into heaven.

El Greco presents us with a painting about the zones of heavenly and earthly life and their relationship to each other. Colour, as much as light, is the key to how this relationship works. In the lower part of the painting, death is accentuated by mourners dressed in black, gathered against a dark backdrop. Announced by the diaphanous vesture of an earthly minister, St Augustine and St Stephen, a bishop and a deacon, two sacred ministers in the celebration of the Eucharist, fill the lower zone, vested in garments of glorious colour.

In the zone above, Christ is seated in majesty at the very apex of the painting. David Davies describes this presentation of him as the radiance of light: 'He is the Sun of Justice. His light is not the light of day, indeed there is no time of day, for this is the plenitude of time.'[1] Here El Greco's use of light seems to anticipate Kandinsky's progress towards abstraction, as white becomes the colour of eternity, not the medium for daylight.

In the vision of heaven, Christ is a figure almost withdrawn from our earthly sight, his vesture blending with the cloud, and a suggestion of receding space behind him. El Greco's use of colour tells us that our vision is through the lens of earthly experience. We see the saints in glorious colour because colour is how their glory in heaven appears to us on earth.

We do, of course, extend this interpretation to the ways we represent the heavenly glory of Christ when seen from an earthly perspective. We use colour because that is also one of the ways in which we interpret the glory of pure light. So the thirteenth-century Franciscan St Bonaventure writes, 'Then Christ will be clothed with all the beauty of the elect as if with a many-coloured tunic [a reference to Joseph the son of Jacob in Genesis 37.3] in which he will shine forth, richly adorned as if covered with all manner of precious stones.'[2]

On earth we cannot see pure light, only its effect. El Greco paints the saints closest to our vision of the miraculous burial in the most vividly coloured vesture; that's what the reflection of glory looks like on earth. Mary, seen in heaven and to whose honour the chapel is dedicated, is similarly depicted in the strong colours of red and blue, traditionally used for the Virgin. These distinctions also suggest how we might understand the phrase 'made white in the blood of the Lamb' in the Revelation of John. To those who, like John, are given a vision of heaven, their robes appear white because that is what characterizes the life of Jesus, the Lamb – the life of God. The redness of blood is an earthly category.

When an artist represents the saints clothed in white, it is a statement of their heavenly vesture and existence, even though this is something that we cannot normally see on earth. The saints painted in glorious colours are being presented to us in earthly colour categories that we also use to define the majesty of heaven. What are we to make of this painting as a statement about our worship and celebration?

At the end of Chapter 3, on fashion, I mentioned that St Paul's has recently been in a partnership to produce new vestments. It has been my privilege to observe the progress of that work and to see at first hand the skill and patience of the Supervisor, Kate Sinton, and her team of volunteers. They have embroidered tiny flowers and delicate crosses. They have fixed crystals, twisted gold and silver thread or plate, and adorned the work with pearls. They have measured silk, cut and assembled cloth and fastened hooks. It has been like watching the working life of another world, illuminated in the pools of the light they needed for their craft. The experience is like underwater exploration, when one's gaze is fixed with greater attention because other senses and distractions are suspended.

The work of these volunteers' hands has produced more than they know. As El Greco suggests in his painting, the vesture of sacred ministers is a statement about the earthly vision of heaven. Vestments are not in themselves sacred or essential, nor do they imply that those who wear them are more important than others. They are a reminder to the ordained of the burden of service they carry and that humility, the Lord's own example, is the only way to carry the burden joyfully and with authenticity.

This is what the final vesting prayer reminds us: 'enable me to bear it so that I may walk in the strength of your grace'. As a theatre critic once observed, 'Heavy, silly or restrictive costumes are important, because they give the wearer a sense of the weight of responsibility of their position.' These costumes in Church also intimate the reality of heaven that words alone cannot convey.

In one of the choruses from *The Rock* T. S. Eliot says that our gaze is submarine. I think this comes sufficiently close to what I want to say about the handiwork of our textile project to justify quotation.

It also connects with how we described the submersion of senses in Kandinsky's transition into abstraction. In all three cases – the textiles, Kandinsky and Eliot – we are seeking the path that takes us to heaven. Submersion is a way of describing this transition; it is the celebratory way of baptism.

Eliot sees, as El Greco, Kandinsky and Gormley also see, that language, verbal or artistic, is orientated towards light as its theme and goal. Unwittingly but accurately, Eliot thereby describes the Carthusian life of the Grand Chartreuse as a model of the celebration of light we all seek:

> We thank Thee for the lights that we have kindled,
> The light of altar and of sanctuary;
> Small lights of those who meditate at midnight
> And lights directed through the coloured panes of windows
> And light reflected from the polished stone,
> And gilded carven wood, the coloured fresco.
> Our gaze is submarine, our eyes look upward
> And see the light that fractures through unquiet water.
> We see the light but see not whence it comes.
> O Light Invisible, we glorify Thee![3]

When in the Chapter 4 we spoke of the threads that we might weave into the hours of our day in order to connect us with heaven, I think that the experience of the skills of the volunteers in our textile project was very much in my mind. It connects what could sound or appear to be flimsy with something much greater. And that is the point of our liturgical celebration as a paradigm of the celebration of life and of heaven. Our individual threads of prayer can be fragile or patchy. Recognized as part of the greater weaving of Eucharistic celebration, the slenderest of them is not insignificant, but contributes to the beauty and efficacious working of the whole.

El Greco's treatment of the Virgin in his vision of heaven may help us to move the identification of vesture away from the role simply of the ordained ministers of the Eucharist. One of the customs that many people may find unusual or even unacceptable is that of clothing a statue of the Blessed Virgin and Christ child with a finely embroidered mantle. In many cases this mantle is as lavishly embroidered as the chasuble that is the over-garment worn by the priest or bishop who celebrates the Eucharist.

The custom of vesting the statue of Our Lady and child is associated with some of the oldest statues that are venerated in the Western Church, particularly in France, at Le Puy, Rocamadour, Vassivière. Nor is it unknown in the restored veneration of Our Lady of Walsingham in England. I think that El Greco's use of colour as narrative for the relationship between earth and heaven illustrates how we account for the use of the mantle on the Madonna and child. It is a statement about our earthly vision of what is true in heaven: that Mary rejoices in the resurrection of her Son (Sun). But I think it also goes deeper.

In Chapter 3, which is on getting dressed, we noted the significance of the skin clothing that God gave to Adam and Eve, and suggested that this clothing symbolized what Mary gave to God in the incarnation. The outdoor garment from which the poncho-like church vestment, the chasuble, is derived was in its original form often made of skins (it also served as a raincoat). So the connection between the vesture of the celebrant of the Eucharist and the transformation of our skin, inherited by Jesus from Mary, strengthens the practice of clothing the statue of Mary and the Christ child with a mantle.

The ancient statues of Mary and the Christ child that I have mentioned belong to a genre of the eleventh and twelfth centuries that are sometimes called the Virgin in Majesty. Even as late in the seventeenth century in the Church of England the recognition of the child on the lap of Mary his mother could elicit veneration.

Mark Frank, Fellow and later Master of Pembroke College, Cambridge, preached an Epiphany sermon in which he notes, 'Here is the shrine and altar, the glorious Virgin's lap, where the Saviour of the world is laid to be adored and worshipped.'[4] The point is that Mary's vesture of glory and majesty is not hers alone or hers by right. It is hers by grace and hers because it is ours. Our flesh and blood, the means by which from her God takes our life to Godself in order to redeem and glorify it, is what accounts for Mary's splendour. Here, again, the principle of representation is at work. One person exemplifies what can, and will be, true of all.

The visual impact of textiles is not, however, the only medium that operates in the liturgical celebration for which they are fashioned. In Chapter 2, on knowledge and nostalgia, we explained this heavenly zone as not known to us, yet one for which we longed. We used Sir Edward Dyer's reference to it as a kingdom in our minds, a place, therefore, of society. Where does this fit in our vision of celebration and liturgical worship?

I think that we have to go back to a detail about Antony Gormley's box of light to identify the way his art illuminates the meaning of Church and churches. Gormley spoke of *Blind Light* as being an inside-out installation. You go into what should be a room in your house, and you find inside a cloud – the weather that belongs outside.

This is an important reversal that we could apply to the nature of church buildings. Not built to define where the presence of God is, with the implication that it is not outside, they in fact operate as a kind of box in which the whole of creation is brought within a space that irradiates what God has made with its true identity: the perfection of heaven. It is in this context that what we believe about the transubstantiation of bread and wine into the body and blood of Jesus makes sense.

This is not a conjuring trick, but a profound revelation of what is real, in the sense that Rowan Williams spoke of art as revealing 'a world that is both new and secretly inscribed in all that is already seen'. Christian celebration inevitably centres on the Church's joyful recognition of the presence of Jesus in her midst. But in the reality of that body, veilingly unveiled beneath the form of bread, we must also see the life of the kingdom of heaven authentically expressed in the life of the one, holy, catholic, apostolic Church of Jesus Christ.

This Church, like the inside-out box of *Blind Light*, brings in all that are outside. It is the full gathering of the human race into life and celebration. Some of the strictest words of Jesus are reserved for those who do not want an inside-out (or, rather, an outside-in) sort of Church:

I tell you, the tax collectors and the prostitutes are going into the kingdom of God ahead of you. For John came to you in the way of righteousness and you did not believe him, but the tax collectors and the prostitutes believed him; and even after you saw it, you did not change your minds and believe him. (Matthew 21.31–32)

So the answer to the question 'Who else is in heaven?' is, we are, though we shall not be properly there until all that God has created has finally arrived. We are not there as visitors or tourists: 'you are citizens with the saints and also members of the household of God' (Ephesians 2.19). Nor are we without the glory of heavenly vesture. The prayers of vesting for celebration point to this sense that for all of us hands, mind and clothing in dignity for life beyond death are the preparation for this eternal reality.

In *The Counsels of Light and Love* the sixteenth-century Spanish mystic, St John of the Cross, a man of disciplined renunciation, like the Carthusians, could nonetheless encourage us to make this extravagant claim in these terms:

With what procrastinations dost thou wait, since thou canst even now love God in thy heart?

Mine are the heavens and mine is the earth; mine are the people, the righteous are mine and mine the sinners; the angels are mine and the Mother of God, and all things are mine; and God himself is mine and for me, for Christ is mine and all for me. What, then, dost thou ask for and seek, my soul? Thine is all this, and it is all for thee.

Consider not thyself as mean, neither pay heed to the crumbs which fall from thy Father's table. Go thou forth from them and glory in thy glory. Hide thee therein and rejoice and thou shalt have the desires of thy heart.[5]

On earth we celebrate this desire and glory with the colours our human differences and experience offer as statements of how we see heaven, here and now. And if we see it in colour, then, Kandinsky-like, we also hear its music.

In Chapter 4 we noted St Augustine's enthusiasm for music and song, and its power as a metaphor for the work of Jesus in liberating us from death. Kandinsky's ability to hear sound in colour presents us with an understanding of how vesture and music integrate in Christian celebration. Just as Pope Paul VI saw the song of the daily Office as a Canticle brought to earth by Jesus, so the colours of the vestments that El Greco sees betoken the sound of heaven on earth. As the colour of these vestments changes to mark the different moods and atmosphere of the mysteries of redemption narrated in time, so the Church's music inevitably will shift its tone.

I suggested that the life of the Grand Chartreuse was like an art installation that modelled eternity. I think its distinctive character does indeed do that, in ways that should illuminate our vision of discipleship lived in the world beyond the cloister. The bridge between Tate Modern and St Paul's Cathedral suggests a similar kind of illumination. Tate Modern, a gymnasium of the imagination, is a good place to prepare for a visit to its neighbour, St Paul's, an installation about heaven. In this baroque, inside-out box, as in every church, cathedral, monastery, convent, or gathered congregation, our hands, mind, dress, and the life that goes beyond the grave combine in celebration of heaven anticipated. I hope that our exploration of these elements of preparation will help to deepen your experience and expectation of what heaven is to be.

Heaven is to be
In God at last made free,
There more and more
Strange secrets of communion to explore:
Within the mighty movements of His will
Our tangled loves fulfil:
To pluck the rosemary we cannot reach
With the mind's span,
And so at last
Breathe the rich fragrance of our hoarded past
And learn the slow unfolding of the plan.
(Evelyn Underhill)[6]

1 Davies, D. (2003), 'El Greco's Religious Art: The Illumination and Quickening of the Spirit', in Davies, D. (ed.), *El Greco*. London: National Gallery Company, p. 52.

2 Bonaventure, 'The Tree of Life', 44, in Cousins, E. (ed.) (1978), *Bonaventure: The Soul's Journey into God; The Tree of Life; The Life of St Francis*. London: SPCK, p. 168.

3 Eliot, T. S. (1963), *Collected Poems*. London: Faber, p. 183.

4 Quoted by Donald Allchin in Allchin, A. M. (1993), *The Joy of All Creation: An Anglican Meditation on the Place of Mary*. London: New City, p. 84.

5 Merton, T. (ed.) (1953), *Counsels of Light and Love of St John of the Cross*. London: Burns and Oates, p. 72.

6 Underhill, E. (1953), 'Thoughts About Heaven', III, in Barkaway, L. and Menzies, L. (eds), *An Anthology of the Love of God: From the Writings of Evelyn Underhill*. London: Mowbray, p. 100.